EASY AS HARD GETS

Jeremy Sims

"There has been a lot of pain this past year. It has not been good for the world, and it has not been good for many people who are dear to me. But our souls do not grow if we insulate ourselves from pain."
Madeleine L'Engle

"We are not on our journey to save the world, but to save ourselves. But in doing that, you save the world."
Joseph Campbell

For Addyson, Carsyn, and Brayden. I see your mom in every smile, laugh, cry, and joy. While you will never know her the way that I did, you know much more than you realize.

(c) 2018 Jeremy Daniel Sims
All Rights Reserved

INTRODUCTION

I didn't set out to write a book. I always wanted to write a book, but that wasn't the intention when I began. All of these words, these stories, these reflections were lived in real time. In the thick of it. And the truth is, I'm still living there. Right in the middle of family meals and morning baths and regimented medicine times and kids' ballgames and church services. Each week I purposed to find a sacred moment of reflection with which to gather all of the words and organize them into a consistent, meaningful something.

Maybe that's all *real* writers do anyway. They gather words and organize them into a consistent something. Every week I would come to my blog and write. I tried to be honest and vulnerable, and yet protect the dignity of my family and especially Tiff. Tiffanni really is the protagonist of this whole thing. She just doesn't have the ability to tell her own story and unfortunately, all of these words are tainted with my perspective, my experience of parts of her story. The only thing that I am certain that I did right is that I kept writing.

At some point, I looked up how many words that I had written. Curiously, I began to google how many words were in other books, other professional, published books- and then I saw it. I had a lot of words and those other books had a lot of words. I had come to the page faithfully and written words on it. And before I realized it, there were a lot of them. Enough in fact that I could bind them into this collection and see it, hold it, smell it. A book.

I can't promise that this book will entertain you or even interest you. What I can promise is that I wrote every word in the thick of it. In the middle of love and joy and sadness and struggle and humanity. And maybe in doing so, my reflections will encourage you in your challenges. Because at the end of the day, we all live there. Some of us, I suppose, write about it on paper, but we all live it. So, thank you for reading my life. I hope and pray that yours is better for it.

STAINED GLASS

I first noticed it in the way she ate. It was as if the food was trying to escape from her fork and she had to bite it before it leapt away. She pounced on it. She would bite the fork so hard that I was afraid that she was going to break her teeth. At first I just thought it was a bad habit. I would say to her, "You sure did bite your fork hard."

"I did?" she would ask.

I was more frustrated by her obliviousness than by her horse habit.

"How can you not hear that? How can you not feel that?"

"I don't know what you're talking about. I'm just eating. Did you have a bad day?"

I used to hate when she did that. It was true, people irritate me more when I've had a long day. I heard some stupid saying when I was younger, "Withdraw from people when one of these things is happening. HALT." It was an acronym for reasons to not be a jerk. When you're Hungry, Angry, L-something and Tired. It was stupid. I hated when she would remind me that it was time to HALT. How about I is for Irritating, why don't I go watch baseball by myself when you're being Irritating.

But then she would smile. Some days it made me mad, some days it melted away every ounce of contention. There was a levity in her smile that couldn't hide her innocence. Her eyes and ears surrendered to her mouth and paid homage by sliding back just right toward the back of her head. It was the most pure emotion indicator that she had. It was jarring the day that she told me that she had a hard time smiling.

"What do you mean?"

"Watch, I can't smile anymore."

"You mean you just don't feel like being happy?"

"No, my face won't smile." And she tried.

How do you tell someone the truth when you hate it as much as they do? How do you tell someone, "You know you're right. Your face isn't smiling? This disease is encroaching on every area of your life?"

So I lied. "What are you talking about? You have just as beautiful of a smile as you ever have." But it wasn't true. The corners of her eyes didn't budge, instead they simply became a fulcrum for a squint.

***

I met Tiffanni at summer camp. I was a camper and she was a counselor, which was odd because I was older than she was. I gladly obeyed her, but only partially. My schoolboy attempt at keeping her attention.

The first day, she went over the rules at the lake. "To ride in a paddle boat, you must always wear a life jacket. To swim in the lake, you must always wear a life jacket. To ride the zipline across the lake, you must always wear a life jacket."

So I wore a life jacket. I just didn't wear it the way it was supposed to be worn. The first day she whistled at me because it looked like I was swimming without a jacket. "Hey you," WHISTLE, "You without the life jacket," WHISTLE. I played dumb. "HEY, you without a jacket," WHISTLE. I finally looked at her to see what all of the commotion was about. She was staring right at me.

I looked behind me, playing dumb. With my eyebrows raised I mouthed, "You mean me?"

"Yes you! You can't swim without a life jacket."

"I'm not. I have a life jacket on." I then turned upside down in the water to reveal the life jacket upside down, legs through the armholes like a diaper. A sumo surprise.

"You have to wear it right," she screamed.

"Oh…sorry." And then she broke. The smile. She didn't smile with her mouth, but her eyes and ears betrayed her. I had won. She noticed me and I would make sure that she noticed me all week at camp. We played the game of counselor and ignorant camper. She constantly correcting my half attempts at following the rules. My ploy, her yielding. My scheme, her give-in. Our first dance.

I debated for several days if I would ask her or not. It felt weird. When I was younger, the entire goal of camp was to ask a girl to the banquet on the last night. Of course, the banquet required dressing up and smelling good. It was the final year that I would ever be a camper. I had just graduated high school and felt the formality of a banquet would define this blossoming relationship in a way that I wouldn't like. The back and forth of the schoolboy romance was so much more fun. It was light, simple and nonchalant. It was giddy. Banquets don't have the ability to be giddy. They require thoughtfulness, but not the stay up all night talking on the phone constantly reassuring that you slept plenty the night before kind of thoughtfulness. Banquets require definition and posturing- a barrage of thought, distracted by thought, "Am I being a gentleman? Is my shirt still tucked in? Is she bored? Should I carry her tray?"- full of thought, just not thoughtful. So I debated. Or maybe I was just nervous.

I didn't ask her to go to the banquet with me. I didn't dress up. I found out later that Tiff was on a break with her long-time boyfriend. I think if I would have asked, the need for definition would have necessitated the conversation and I wasn't confident enough to handle that love triangle.

We exchanged glances all night. Mine held expectation and heat. Hers seemed to hold whimsy and carefree. Thoughtfully, I was falling in love.

***

"You look comfortable," the server said. I hadn't even noticed that my legs were criss-cross applesauce. However odd it is for a grown man to sit so comfortably in a restaurant booth, it had been lost on me. I had kicked off my flip-flops and sat leaning forward. My shins had been kicked so many times over the last two years since her diagnosis that I had to figure out a new way to sit.

I've found that the body will adjust to comfortable once it realizes that this is going to be a trend. When I was sixteen years old, I thought that driving with both hands at two and ten was lame, so I learned to drive with one hand at 12 o'clock. I usually propped the other arm out the window. For the first week my entire right side was sore, but my body adjusted. It became easy and even comfortable to drive lean-cocked with one shoulder floating in mid air in order to portray cool while the other shoulder sat against the backrest. So, after being kicked in the shins and accidentally grimacing every time, I had to come up with another plan. Tiffanni apologized each time. It was painful, not the kick, but that she couldn't control it and yet felt the need to apologize after each infraction. Why did she have to apologize? I hate that feeling.

"I'm so sorry."

"For what?"

"I kicked you. I saw your face."

"No you didn't. What are you talking about?"

"I hate this. Why don't we just go home. You didn't have to

take me out. I'm embarrassed to be out anyway. Let's just go."

"No, you're doing great. It didn't even hurt. You know that I have no pain tolerance. You're the one who had all of the babies. I think I would have just had Addyson and given up."

"No you wouldn't, you love our kids!"

"Of course I love our kids… because you had them." We laughed. It was always my sense of humor that she was attracted to anyway. If you ask ten girls what they want most in a man, nine of them will say a good sense of humor. She had to like my sense of humor. What else would she have done with that perfect smile?

We stayed and we laughed and I sat criss-cross applesauce and she was none the wiser.

***

We sat across from our friends. This was our very first double date and Brad and Leslie had asked us to go out. "You two have so much fun. Come show us how to have fun," Leslie had asked Tiffanni. Coincidentally, Brad and Leslie had been dating the same amount of time that Tiffanni and I had- one year.

When Tiffanni told me, I said to her, "How in the world are we supposed to train that boring couple how to do anything?" Leslie was as bland as a communion wafer and Brad a sex fiend. Either they had a secret life of raucous religion or this wasn't going to last anyway. I agreed.

Chili's is a place for lovers. It was mine and Tiffanni's first date ever and our first double date one year later. Something about the guacamole. Brad and Leslie stared at us while Tiffanni controlled the conversation. She was brilliant at any party. I've always found it odd that she, an introvert, could be so mesmerizing in a social setting. Maybe it was the Mango Iced Tea. Leslie finally inserted, "Tell us how to be fun. You two are so fun. Tell us."

There are moments when you know that you've made a great decision about your future and then there are these moments. They stand sublime in a trophy case of the mind. Markers that one can recall and use as energy and determination in harder moments. Rarely are they planned or expected, but they present themselves with such clarity that even in the very same instant, the significance is obvious. Tiffanni looked at me and I at her. I saw her eyebrow raise the very slightest and then her nose flared. It was too much for me and we both laughed at each other. She laughed open mouthed that started with a muffled "Ha". It sounded like a Wynton Marsalis muted trumpet. It got me so tickled that I blew out a laugh between my lips. They flapped, with the fully air-loaded cheeks, just like I could have played her trumpet. Somehow I spit in her face and she laughed even more. The question, the moment, the laugh, the spit- Wynton would be hard pressed to create a more beautiful song.

***

We sit across from her neurologist. Our general practitioner recommended him when Tiffanni finally said, "Something has to be wrong. I can't keep my balance. I shake at weird times and keep forgetting things." He talks in a language that he somehow expects us to both understand. At this point, we only understand shock. There are words that are impossible to explain without an experiential frame of reference. This is one of those words- surreal. A surreal moment is a moment that plays back the same way that it is experienced, in slow motion. Behind the doctor is a bookshelf filled with periodicals. There is a shelf filled with dozens of *Journal of Neurological Sciences*. Today they are as useful as giving a starving man a picture of food. There are six certificates on his wall and a picture of what seems to be the doctor forty years younger. It is in black and white. He is a handsome man and smiles as if he has accomplished a lot in the picture. He poses as he shakes the hand of someone in pristine regalia, yet he can't even get Tiffanni's hand to stop shaking. All of the letters and all of the certificates, all of the Journals and the fancy office at the end of the hall- crap.

He wishes us well as we follow him down the hall. He hands us five prescriptions and three starter sample packs. We leave the office, hands filled with a concoction of hope. "We'll try different combinations of these until we get it right," he says.

I want to scream at him, "She's not a lab rat. This is our life that we're trying to 'get right!'" But nothing comes out. I smile in response and shake his feckless hand with my own. A duo of death. We will accompany her to the end with little more to help than our smiles.

***

We lay in bed that first night. Not the first night of our lives together, the first night of the rest of our life together.

"I'm gonna die."

"No you're not, don't say that."

"I am going to die."

"Stop saying that."

"I can't play games with you tonight. I'm going to die and I need you to say it back to me."

"I won't say it because it's not going to happen. I mean it. Don't say it again."

"I'm not scared. Don't be scared."

I don't know how to respond to this. Does she need me to be strong or does she need to be strong for me?

***

She's so kind to everyone. We can't go anywhere that she doesn't say something nice to someone. I hate that it embarrasses me. I used to pray for a miracle, but what's the point? The truth is that I've seen a miracle. This disease not only affects movement but it also affects mood, yet somehow, she is as bright and positive as I have ever experienced her. It doesn't make sense.

"You sure look pretty today," she says to the lady wiping the table next to us. I look over my shoulder and see her nametag that reads, "Betsy."

Betsy turns around and then realizes that Tiffanni is staring right at her, her face brightens with curiosity. "Thank you baby, you look pretty yourself."

"You're doing such a great job. Thank you for working so

hard." Tiffanni's broken speech dismisses any interpretation of insincerity and I can tell that Betsy is warming. Faces are undeniable. Words, actions, and even tone have this chameleon quality of control. But faces, they give away the lot. Betsy seems to have that look of being on candid camera, but Tiffanni's erratic movements are surprisingly disarming. Betsy's closed-mouth smile now reveals her teeth and I now know that Tiffanni has melted suspicion.

The darkest thing this disease has determined to do, to be, is eradicated by a gentle exchange between two humans. It's funny what being stripped of dignity does to a person. It would seem that there is a finite amount of dignity in the world. The more Tiffanni loses, the more she discovers in others.

***

"Wait, I can't breathe, you're going too fast." She brings her hands to her face and cups around her nose.

"I'm so sorry, I got caught up daydreaming." I chuckle and she smiles.

"No big deal, you're just going to drown me." I finger through her hair to see if all of the shampoo has been rinsed. When it's been a long day, I don't allow this time together to be special. I hurry through. The routine never varies, just my timing. Shampoo in the hair, I let it sit to do its work, although, I'm not sure what it's doing. I then squeeze body wash onto the loufa, the washcloth we first used would never lather enough to feel like she was getting clean. I begin to wash her back, then her arms. For some reason, everytime that I begin to wash her arm, it flies into the air. It is an unforced reflex. It reminds me of a baby being awakened from a nap and throwing his hands into the air. Balance, disorientation, I don't know, but Tiffanni's hands always fly when I wash her arms. I sometimes think that her body believes that it has to constantly remind me of its lack of control. "Wait, we'll do your armpits next." And she looks at her arm like it is detached from her body. "I didn't do that on purpose."

"I know sweetie." The soapy water runs down her back.

"Ok, now your armpits," and I run the blade down her underarms. My knees usually begin to hurt about this time. My legs cramp and I hurry the process. "Close your eyes." I rinse out her hair and skin and now her body matches her soul.

Dressing is always interesting. I towel her off and she stands exposed. There was a time this was a sensual moment. I never noticed the transition from companion to caretaker, it just happened one day. Her beautiful body, once exciting and erotic now feels like the other parts that are exposed throughout the day.

Because I didn't register the biting the fork as anything more than a bad habit, I wasn't looking for her coordination to fail either. She had always been clumsy. Those legs had marks all over them. I used to ask her if she shaved with a machete. Now I towel them off. On my knees, she stares down at me as I dry off the bruises on her legs. Too many to remember the how. The light from the ceiling fixture behind her casts a silhouette. I look up at her and from the light beyond her I see a prism made up of the colors of beauty and pain, loss and grief, helplessness and love, hope and death. And she smiles.

WE PLANTED PECAN TREES

My parents have been married 42 years and raised four kids, naturally, I am one of them. Growing up wasn't perfect- why do we even say that? Like that is a criteria that can be met. God doesn't even use the term perfect for creation. He says, "It is good." And that is how I grew up. It was good. We moved several times and I always had built in playmates. We were creators, dreamers, explorers. Sticks, and rocks, and balls, and rope were the brushes that painted our adventures. More than once my siblings hung from trees by their feet, sledded down our backyard on trashcan lids and car hoods, designed and built castles, survived b-b-gun wars, swam with alligators, and created new sports. It was good.

All of us discovered our personalities and gifts in the safety and stability of a good home. I'm lucky. I told my parents that I wanted to be a doctor, a lawyer, an FBI agent, and a pastor. They always said the same thing, "Great. Work hard." They came to ball games, concerts, plays, took us to church, vacations, camping, art exhibitions, school projects, I grew up good. I know this is trite, but I never wondered about my family. I never questioned my parents' love. Stability and safety do that.

So it didn't surprise me when my dad called a year after Tiffanni was diagnosed with Huntington's. He was matter-of-fact. He needed to be, I was living in a fog (and still do a lot). "You know things aren't going to get better right?" he asked me. "Your mom and I have decided to quit our jobs and come help you with Tiff and the kids. The kids need stability and safety. We'll help you with that." And that was it.

Huntington's is ugly. It's slow, and long, and painful to watch, I can only imagine that it's worse to experience. It affects movement, mood, and cognition. I've noticed over the last four and a half years that every 6-12 months, Tiff takes a step back. It was eating at first. She couldn't hold her fork. So we ate things she could hold like chicken fingers and sandwiches and corndogs and cookies- boy, does she love cookies. But then she couldn't bring the food to her mouth. Her hands wouldn't cooperate. Then it was bathing. Lately it's walking. She struggles to do the routine. So we help- all of us.

My dad and I just finished building a house a few months ago that suits our family and lifestyle well. We've worked on other stuff for the outside lately. By we, I mean my dad. He just finished building a beehive- I guess it's not the actual hive, he's not God, but it's a beehive house. He finished a chicken coup this weekend for our 10 Rhode Island Reds. Apparently they lay the best eggs and are the easiest to keep up with- who knows, I'm not a farmer. Next week he'll plant the garden. It's a natural transition for my dad after tilling the soil of souls for over twenty years. A couple of weeks ago he came home with pecan trees in the back of the truck. About 6' tall and maybe an inch in circumference.

"What are these," I asked, shovel in hand.

"Pecan trees."

"Yeah, that's great! I love pecan pies."

"You get that from me." He got down on his knees and broke the dirt around the roots that were trapped in a pot- simple tributaries that would grow into strong rivers. "It doesn't hurt that your mom makes the best."

"So, how long until we get to make pecan pies with our pecans?" I asked.

"Oh, about 10-15 years," he said, like that wasn't a lifetime.

"Fifteen years!?"

He laughed. "You going anywhere?"

"I like pecan pies, so I guess not."

"Well, Me neither."

CRYING OVER SPILLED MILK

It was fajitas and a hamburger at Chili's on that first one back in 1996- you know Chili's- the restaurant for lovers. "Always date each other," we were told, so I just assumed everyone else did. At least once a week, almost religiously, for 20 years Tiffanni and I have dated. Chili's, ball games, picnics, food courts, movies, ballets, drive-ins, state parks, the theater, concerts, day drives, Christmas light looking, lakes, malls, lots of dang malls [sigh], Walmarts, skating rinks, museums, we dated. It was always my job to be the date planner. I think I assumed the role and went with it. I need variety and choices by personality, so dates were always an adventure. From geo-caching at a state park to an NHL Hockey game on our first anniversary (not sure what I was thinking), a random adventure was always a possibility.

Dates have changed a little lately. We still do them, but the random has turned in to the routine. Not out of boredom or laziness, but out of simplicity and necessity. There are only so many things that you can do with our mobility challenges, and quite possibly, I think we turned old overnight. So Fridays are Date Days and it's Dairy Queen and a movie. Not some

Fridays, every Friday. Dairy Queen offers the convenience of close proximity to the movies (where we get our variety) and Tiffanni loves the chicken fingers. To be honest, I eat the average food to get to dessert. We love our blizzards.

A few weeks ago we were at Dairy Queen and a couple of older ladies noticed us. I thought they were staring because I was feeding Tiffanni each bite (which is pretty common- both), but finally one looked at me and said, "Is your name Jeremy?" I responded with, "Yes", to which they began to tell me about their church that I happened to preach in a few months before. They said they enjoyed it, but really, is there anything else that you could say sitting at the next table at Dairy Queen? "Listen Jeremy, you're going to have to step it up. You can't exegete scripture very well and you need some help closing- like do it a lot sooner." So we chatted about the church and my family. Eventually, as old people do, they asked the inevitable question. "If you don't mind me asking, what's wrong with Tiffanni?"

The truth is that I don't mind people asking. I don't really care what their motives are, nosiness or concern, I'll answer. So I told them about Huntington's Disease which neither of them had heard of before. "It's an ugly neurodegenerative disorder that affects movement, mood, and cognition." We talked a bit more and heard several additional, "Bless your hearts," and continued our meal. Finally the big payoff came and they delivered our blizzards. The best part of the whole day. My mouth watered as they turned the blizzard upside down to show me how secure and cold it was. I always think, "Just put it down. If it falls out we're going to have to sit here while you go make another one." They placed Tiffanni's oreo blizzard in front of her and my salted caramel truffle blizzard in front of me. My stomach growled and my taste buds pulsed. Just as I picked up the spoon, I heard the inevitable words from behind me, "Would you mind if we prayed for you?"

Look, I'm a preacher. I always want prayer, but something about the white hair and buns told me that this wasn't going to be a short, "God bless them."

"Sure," I said. And they gathered around our table and placed their hands on us. And they prayed. And they prayed some more. And they kept praying. It wasn't loud, but it was long. So long. Tears, tongues, and taking turns, they covered everything that you can think of. When they ran out of English, they didn't run out of praying. I get it. Some people have to do something. Some people have to try to help alleviate our pain or their own emotional dissonance. In my world it's usually prayer. Sometimes it's more tangible things, but people do stuff. They have to.

After what felt like forever, the ladies wiped their tears, wrapped their grandmother arms around us, and said, "Goodbye, we'll be praying for you." And in my most human of moments, I looked down at the table and noticed my own tear well up in my eye. The result of our prayer, two melted puddles of blizzard.

THE MAYOR OF NOWHERE

I live foggy and numb a lot lately. A few years ago, my counselor told me that my body was doing important work. "Bodies are smart. They have a shutdown mechanism so that you don't feel everything that you experience. If you did, some days would be too much." So I live foggy, a lot. Thanks, body. The good news is that I don't have extreme lows. The downside is that the pendulum doesn't swing very far the other way either. I live in the middle. A hammock instead of a tilt-a-whirl. I used to get so excited, like a kid, when I was doing something new. Christmas morning, going to Six Flags, riding a motorcycle or in a convertible, a dinner party, a Giants' game- they all surged my emotions. Now, I tell myself, "Self, you would normally get excited about this, so be present to this moment. It really is spectacular."

However, there is an exception.

Art.

Art gets me. It grabs me and reads me and understands me. It tells my story and feels my feelings. It communicates what I don't quite have the words for. It doesn't have to alleviate my pain, it expresses it for me. Art holds the key to my unlocked emotions and when I give it its required space, it gladly opens the door. It's not just me- it's you too. But art has an enemy. Its arch nemesis is hurry. Art is a foreign language which requires that I spend time with it to understand it. It is not my native tongue, so I must work with it, study it, hone my understanding of it. To skim a fiction book or worse, to keep my cell phone distraction next to me while I read, to walk flippantly through a museum, to fast-forward a movie, to text during a play is to blaspheme art. Art is a jealous friend that requires full attention. My friends have become accustomed to my distracted focus, but art isn't as gracious. For art to breathe, for it to inhale and exhale blood and life, it must have undivided attention. For art to incite my imagination and stimulate my rusty feelings, I have to yield my pace. Hurry, multi-tasking, working hard and getting things done quickly has its place, just not with art. The true artist has the ability to highlight what I wouldn't normally see and tell me why it's important. I don't see that if I'm in a rush. My receptors are inhibited by hurry.

My culture is an art killer. But Tiffanni, she is my artist nurturer. I can't brush her teeth too quickly or she'll get cavities. I can't feed her too quickly or she'll choke. I can't walk fast or she'll trip. I can't talk too fast or she gets lost. I can't do her makeup too quickly or she'll look like a clown. Trust me, I've learned the hard way. She forces me to slow down. She causes me to rethink my schedule and adjust my day to remove the events that don't matter so that I have enough time for the things that do. Some days I sit in between bites and think, "I'm here doing nothing in nowhere."

As she encourages my art appreciation through her tempered

pace, she loses hers. She can't read anymore. Can't understand music. Can't keep up with movies. Can't stay still for the theater. So, sometimes we do nothing and sit Nowhere. We eat blizzards and sit quietly. We ride in the car, quietly. We sit on the back porch, quietly- and she makes space for me to visit Nowhere.

Hurry escorts me to places that are detrimental to my soul, my family, and my relationships. To un-hurry is to go Nowhere. And it is Nowhere that art makes its home. Art, the antidote to my foggy life. And there in Nowhere Tiffanni is the uncontested mayor. Others campaign for the attention of hurry, workaholism, multi-tasking, and noise. Not Tiff- she is content to lead her quaint little city. When I visit, my world slows and my busy-satiated mind calms. My attention is drawn to the beauty that escapes the rushed. The mayor helps dissipate the fog. And you wouldn't want anyone else running this city, trust me.

LIFE AT BOTH ENDS

I refuse to call it a man crush. I'm pretty sure that I've watched everything that Aaron Sorkin has ever written. The Big Screen- *Malice, A Few Good Men, The American President* (which paved the way for the greatest TV series of all time.) *Charlie Wilson's War, The Social Network, Moneyball,* and *Steve Jobs.* I've seen on the Small Screen *Sports Night, Studio 60 on the Sunset Strip, The Newsroom,* and…drumroll…*The West Wing.* As a matter of fact, I'm watching the series through for my third time now. Nothing compares. All that other stuff on television plays second fiddle to his Magnum Opus.

I love *The West Wing,* and all of Sorkin's work, in part because of his idealism. He's a romantic. He's an optimist and in him I find a kindred spirit. He convinces me in every episode that the government, yes the government, can be a force of good and service and justice in the world. If Josiah Bartlet were running for president today, he'd win in a landslide- not that his competition this year lends itself to a convincing argument against his brilliance.

I'm a romantic. At least, I think that I am. Yet, at the same time- my life isn't cooperating right now. Somehow in a romantic's world, the boy always gets the girl, the cop always saves the day, good wins, evil loses, love prevails, Heath Ledger is knighted as Sir William in *A Knight's Tale*, Meg and Tom fall in love in every single movie together, Sadness and Joy work together to give Riley this complex emotional and fulfilling life, and Jed Bartlet is president forever.

But that's the movies. The difficulty with being a romantic in a difficult life is the temptation to deny reality. In fact, denial is part of the grieving process. So, I tip toe this line between romanticism and finding "the beauty in the sorriness of life." I know how this ends. I drive by the nursing home where my mother-in-law died from this disease every day of my life. On the right side of the road is the nursing home, and on the left side of the road is the house that Tiffanni and I built together. Brayden was born there. My kids have a treehouse still there. We celebrated Christmases, Trick-or-treated, hunted Easter eggs, all three kids began Kindergarten there. We barbecued, hosted New Year's Eve parties, we lived there. A tunnel of grief. Death on one side and nostalgia on the other.

But it's the drive. I leave my new house where our beautiful children laugh, and play, and dream, and live. We have pecan trees, and chickens, and bees, and our Golden Retriever, Fortinbras. And I make my way to the places that form my kids, and encourage them, and breathe dreams into them. I drive through the shadow of death every day, on my way from life and to life. From our home of safety and personality nurturing on our way to their school and our church, we pass through the tunnel of grief only to hope again.

I'm a romantic. And the beauty of the drive isn't the death in the middle of the journey, it's the life at both ends. Death doesn't have the first word and it won't have the last.

BROKEN BODIES

There's this story in scripture where a woman had a bleeding problem for twelve years. Non-stop bleeding, every day of her life. What we don't get is her backstory. The Levitical law prohibited her from ever associating with other people. She was considered unclean. A disease she couldn't control, she didn't cause, she didn't deserve, and yet her greatest punishment- she was left alone to deal with it by herself. So twelve years this lady had no friends, no family, no community. She never went to church, never went to the store, never got out in public, never went to a family reunion. She was secluded from relationship and banished to solitude.

Which makes it surprising that this miracle even happens. Jesus's words, "Who touched me?" carry with it not just a question but an indictment. Who? Every human desires to be known- fully known. And she was an unknown nobody. Of course he said, "Who?" No one knew who she was. For twelve years. Her healing carried more than a physical cure- it initiated community restoration. Most can deal with any problem, any sickness, any loss, as long as they can work through their grief in community. This unnamed lady lived in solitary confinement. Until Jesus healed her. I can only suppose that the greatest healing wasn't her body, but the restoration of her relationships.

I usually get stuck on the stage when we have communion at our church. We need background music for most experiences in the church and I orchestrate the mood- the Mood Maestro. Wedding music, baby dedication music, water baptism music, altar music- there's a song to go along with each component. So I stand on the stage and sing with my musician and vocalist friends.

The beauty of communion is that we share it together. The bread and wine represent Jesus's body and blood. That he's there too. So when we take it, we remind ourselves that as we do this together, we're only here, together, because Jesus is there too. It's regularly a solemn moment- introspective and sacred. It's a beautiful ceremony that embodies and symbolizes the brilliance of Jesus's sacrifice. We share His broken body and together are made whole.

Tiffanni isn't able to sit up during church anymore because she moves so erratically. So my mom bought her a pillow and she sprawls out in the pew. We have a routine on Sunday mornings- she comes in and drinks her smoothie out of her indestructible Starbucks cup and then lays down for the remainder of the service. When I lead worship, I can see her face. Her body fidgets, her arms flail, and she rubs a carpet burn into her knees from the burlapped pew upholstery. I'm requesting a silk pew. But then again, we'd just slip-n-slide right on to the floor.

The other night we shared communion. We sang a song about the blood of Christ. The other pastors distributed what we call "the elements." Jay asked if everyone had been served. Mark came and prayed over the time and just before we were about to eat the bread, I looked and saw her knee. It was just above the top of the pew. Jerking, scabbed, frail- her knee. With everyone in the room prepared to put a piece of wafer in their mouths, she laid there, outside of the community. Her broken body forbidding her to share in the broken body of Christ. Possibly, the person who needed to feel a part of the community more than any of us. Ostracized and isolated she laid there alone.

So I did what any of you would have done. I walked off of the stage and helped her rejoin the community. Her community. People who have pledged their love to her and our family. To see this through with us whatever the future holds. And we took the bread, and we took the juice, and I helped her broken body ingest the broken body of Christ along with the rest of us broken parts of the body. Her family. Her community.

NIGHT TERRORS

I walked through the house at 2am. It was at least the second time that I checked on the kids that night, not counting praying for them and saying goodnight before bed. My mind was doing mean things. I had played over in my mind what I would do if one of them wasn't breathing, if something was wrong. I went through my CPR steps, was it five chest compressions or ten?

About a year before Tiffanni was diagnosed in 2011, my subconscious starting "doing work" the counselor would later tell me. Something was wrong in my family and my mind played games with all of the possibilities. So many people told me later, "We knew something was wrong, we just didn't know how to tell you." So my mind toyed with my emotions and fear crept in.

So many people know me as happy and fun, but nights were terrifying. Endless outcomes of pain haunted my imagination. One of my children dying was the worst. I have no doubt that every parent fears this. But for me, it was out of character. So every night I couldn't fall asleep until I checked on the kids multiple times. I began to lose sleep, walking back and forth to their rooms just to make sure they were ok. I would tell myself, "If you don't go check on them now and they die in the night, you'll find them in the morning and regret for the rest of your life that you could have done something." So, I would get up and check on them- over and over. Every night for months.

I even became superstitious about prayer. Fear does this. I thought that if I didn't pray for my kids each night at bedtime and say the mantra, "God protect my kids," that somehow there was a greater chance that something would happen. It became part of the routine- prayer for protection, and then I would double check that God was doing his part throughout the night, since I had done mine. I pretended like it was normal. Or maybe I just didn't let myself think about it.

I was in the middle of my doctoral studies and taking a class on counseling. One of our requirements was to work through a current problem with our teacher. I couldn't point to anything to talk about, when it struck me, I guess I could talk to him about the fear for my family, how many times I check on the kids at night. Maybe it's not normal.

So, we talked. One of the most amazing things that a professional can do is make you feel normal. Not that what I was doing was normal, but it was human. There are moments of our lives that things get out of balance and we don't even realize it. He told me, "What you're doing isn't healthy, but it's not surprising. You're a parent."

I asked him, "What should I do?" I expected wisdom. I anticipated that he would look deeply into my childhood and diagnose some stunted maturation process. Like I slept with a nightlight too long as a child or watched *Jaws* too early in my adolescent development. What he told me was frustrating.

"You've got to stop."

"Stop what?" I asked.

"Stop checking on your kids at night."

"What do you mean I have to stop? Like, I just don't do it anymore? That's all you're going to tell me?"

"Yes, that's it. What you're doing is normal, in that it's common. It's just not healthy. So stop."

And that was it. That was my professional. Sometimes things don't need complicated answers. The first night was miserable. I fought all night. I dreaded waking them up the next morning and throughout the night projected horrors into that moment. But there they were, sound asleep, sun peeking through the windows, wadded up in a comforter. Alive. So, I did it again the next night. I don't think it was any easier. But I stayed with it. I gave in once in a while and graciously chided myself. Doesn't every addict relapse at least once? I don't remember when it went away. I just know that I don't feel that same fear anymore. Sure, some nights are a little harder, but I can't live that way again.

I don't check on my kids at night any more. Although I pray with Addyson, Carsyn, and Brayden every night, I don't ever ask for protection. I can't go back there. I can't live in a world where everything bows to my fear, even God. I can't worry about breaking a mirror, seeing a black cat, opening an umbrella inside, or checking the protection box off during my prayers. I've taken my step of faith toward a God who loves me, my children, and Tiffanni more than I do with a perfect love. And perfect love casts out all fear.

NEXT BEST LAID PLANS

Organization was never my gift. It was Tiff's. I'll bring the adventure and Tiff can get us packed. As odd as it sounds, I just started packing my own bags for trips three years ago. And the truth is that I sometimes get some help from family friends for that. Trying to remember to pack enough socks and deodorant sends me into my reptilian brain- fight or flight. So I fly.

This past weekend I planned this amazing backpacking experience for me and the kids. A 14-Mile journey along the Pinhoti Trail in the Talladega National Forest. It's a trip that I've taken several times with teenagers and know very well. We hike in 2 miles, stay at a campsite, hike 10 miles, stay at a campsite, and then hike out 2 miles to the car- a three day journey through God's Country. That 10-miler is a killer, but I thought the kids could make it.

I left my car at the end point, got a ride from a pastor friend from Eastaboga (a real city) to the starting point- Sweetwater Lake. A nice hike beside the lake and into the woods for 2 miles and we were off. No complaints, easy trek, just fun. I breathed in the mountain air and thought, I just don't do this enough.

The kids were enjoying themselves, I kept asking, "Do you love this or what?!" They always responded excitedly. I can't tell if they really do like backpacking or just loved being on a new adventure with me- but who cares. It was amazing.

We got to our campsite quickly, set up the tent, and went crawfish searching. The water was cool and refreshing after a warm walk- not ideal for backpacking, but perfect nonetheless.

One of the problems with hiking in the heat is that all of the other critters that need the sun come out to play too. After our creek walk, I spent 20-minutes picking ticks off of all of us. Ticks suck. Not to mention, I had to keep an eye out for snakes, which we nearly tripped over on our hike in. Snakes bite. But all was made well by my selection in snacks.

Tiff never let me go grocery shopping. My stomach had this way of dictating what I would buy in light of the list that I had been tasked with. I'd go for milk and butter and return with Ben and Jerry's Chocolate Cookie Dough ice cream and a yo-yo, only to be sent back out for a second run to the store for milk and butter. I kept the yo-yo. Lately, I have no inhibitors on my grocery store purchases. I buy what I want, gain a little weight and a cavity, and eat my fill of sweets. Lucky for my children, my mom does the vast majority of the grocery shopping and meal planning.

But not this time. I'm a snacker, so we had snacks. You have to have calories to burn for the 10-mile hike! I bought chocolate covered granola bars (is that an oxymoron?), decadent trail mix, nutter butters, chips ahoy, oreos, gummy bears, ritz pb crackers, and peanut butter M&M's. Did I mention, I'm a snacker? Around 6pm the snacks had burned through and the kids were ready to eat. They were so excited about eating our freeze dried meals that we brought- spaghetti, lasagna, or chicken and rice. To be honest, the meals are much better than you think. I was so hungry. The way the meals work, you boil water and simply add. Easy as that.

We each selected our meal for the evening. There was even a picnic table at our campsite, 2 miles in the forest. I opened my well planned backpack to get the JetBoil (a piece of equipment to boil water rapidly.) Organization was never my gift. It was Tiff's. I'll bring the adventure and Tiff can get us packed. I feel like I had done my part- we were having so much fun! Hiking, snakes, tick removal, creek walks, we played cards, I-Spy, it was brilliant! Except, I couldn't find the JetBoil. You know, the most important piece of equipment that we had. I looked up at the kids, staring in anticipation of dinner and fed them the news- "I forgot the JetBoil."

Brayden began to cry. Ungrateful kid. Addyson just walked off. Passive Aggressive child. Carsyn told me it was ok that I was so careless because she "didn't want me to feel bad." Meh. And like that, I relinquished my Dad of the Year title.

I quickly gathered the troops and Winston Churchill'd my way through. "Good news and bad news. The good news is that we have food. It's crap, but we won't starve. The bad news is that we're 12 miles from the car and we don't have an option- in the morning we're hiking to the car. It'll take all day, but you can do it." And with that, we started joking and having fun again. Kids are resilient. Adaptable. What a great way to make a memory- *Remember that time we went backpacking and almost starved to death.* If I had the ability to plan, I might have designed the oversight.

We slept well and hit the trail at 8am. Full of granola bars and

M&M's, we hiked. And it was beautiful. The kids were amazing. No complaining, just enjoying one another. We talked, and laughed, and played, and I loved every minute of it.

Several times along the way, I couldn't help but think, *This wasn't the way I planned it.* We were supposed to do this together. I bring the adventure and you pack. I'll lasso the world, you just tell me what to do with it. But those were the best laid plans, and plans change.

DANCING AND CRYING

My brother was married this weekend. Adam said, "I do" to the woman of his dreams and they were married in this quaint, rustic warehouse that was filled with life and love on Sunday. It was a perfect weekend. One of those weekends that the air determines to explode with rain, but realizes that there is something important happening, so it acquiesces. It finally let go during the ceremony that was indoors and stopped again just in time for all of the guests to leave. Mother Nature, the romantic.

As guests entered they received their order of service from the three most gorgeous greeters (Addyson, Carsyn, and Sophia.) The troop of family and friends signed a globe, recommendations of travel for the couple-to-be, and got their seats.

The ceremony was beautiful. Both dads were ministers and officiated. The bride and groom read their vows to each other and exchanged rings. They shared communion and each dad spoke a blessing over the couple- which I wish was possible to be a part of every wedding ever. I do's, a kiss, and forever.

I love late weddings because it always means better food and more fun. Everyone loosens up when the sun sets. We ate and watched Adam and Keri cut the cake. We made toasts and speeches and "To Adam and Keri's".

After all of the traditional pomp, the party hit the dance floor. Keri had asked for 80's and 90's pop- all night. Whitney Houston, Journey, Wilson Phillips, with some Etta James and Louis Armstrong sprinkled in. Couples jumped and lip synced to "Faithfully" and "Hold On For One More Day." When they weren't bouncing, they were arm in arm swaying. But I didn't have anyone to dance with. The odd part of the day was feeling both emotions. Life rarely gives us a single, undiluted emotion. I watched as my brother made his vows of "for better or worse, rich or poor, sickness or health," and eyed my Tiff in the corner. A body that refused to cooperate the way the weather had.

The excitement of the future, with all of the hopes of tomorrow- the uncertainty made thrilling because of the fact that you aren't doing it alone. Life and love and hope and family. The best of what it means to be human. And yet I straddled over a chasm of ambiguity.

So my sister asked me to dance. And I felt both horizons of the night. The emotions crashed over me as I watched my kids dance and laugh and Tiff struggle to keep her head up and her arms still. My sister didn't tell me why her cheek was stained with tears, but what other reason would you be asked by your sister to dance at a wedding? And I whispered into her ear, "Thank you for being sad with me." As she too, teetered between the shores of emotions.

So we danced and cried. My brother in one eye, my bride in

the other. Because this is and isn't the way things are supposed to be. Because Vows hold both halves of the human experience. Because the rhythm of humanity beats to joy and pain. Because dancing is beautiful and sacred, and so is crying.

THE LAST RIDE

Tiffanni and I were married in January of 1999. The plan was to make sure that we did it over a break so that our college friends could come and we could go back to school for the spring semester. But I overloaded my schedule and finished early. 20+ hours at school, 25 hours a week at Red Lobster, For the Seafood Lover in You, and threw in some baseball so I wouldn't have to sleep at all.

January is the worst time to get married. Not that it matters on the wedding day, but there are so many limited options for anniversary get-aways in the years that follow. A few years ago we decided to spend a few nights in Chattanooga, only to return after one because they shut down the city for a blizzard (the Southern kind- ice and wind chill.) But January it was. It made sense eleven months earlier when we started planning the festivities. A lot happens in eleven months.

I like surprises, so I told Tiffanni to pack warm for the honeymoon and that's all of the hints that she got. We went on a cruise to the Bahamas and back to Orlando for a couple of nights. We stayed in the Wilderness Lodge at Disney and then went to Animal Kingdom. Tiff and I had been to every park in the area except Disney's Theme Park Zoo, so we gave it a shot. And true to Disney, it was brilliant.

Over the next 17+ years, we made a life of hitting theme parks. Vacations and excursions were planned around roller coasters- The Magic Kingdom, Hollywood Studios, Epcot, Universal Studios, Six Flags, Alabama Adventures, Busch Gardens, Sea World Orlando, Sea World San Diego, Disney Quest, Point Mallard, White Water Atlanta- we like theme parks.

Last week we went on our Summer Vacation with Tiff's side of the family to Orlando. There's eleven of us. I know, because there are no 11-person configurations of dinner tables that work well. Someone gets stuck on the end and I knee-joust with them all night.

Last year, Jay and I took the kids to Aquatica, a water park, while my in-laws took Tiffanni and Stacey shopping. It just seemed like Tiffanni couldn't do theme parks anymore. She moves so much that the heat is unbearable and I knew that she couldn't walk around a park anymore. So for the last several months, Tiffanni begged to go to Disney. She told me, "We're going."

There aren't many things in life worse than telling your partner, "No." I never bought into the subordination theory of marriage- we were partners and made decisions together. Some things I was good at and needed to make the call on, some things she was, but mostly we made decisions together. That whole your husband is the head thing, that actually stems from the curse of sin (Genesis 3:16), and I'd prefer to not subject myself to curses if I can. So, we partnered. But lately, I have to say, "No," a lot. It doesn't feel right and I hate it.

So I avoided talking about it with Tiffanni all week in Orlando. I thought that if I pretended that it wasn't an option that it would just go away. And she pestered. "I want to go. Can we please go?"

On the next to last night, my mother-in-law and I talked and agreed it was just too hard. It wouldn't work and Tiffanni just couldn't make it. I went to bed sad. So many parts of this disease take from you without warning. You don't realize that it's the last time to do something until it's over. But to my surprise, I woke to a text from my mother-in-law that just said, "Let's do it. We'll make it work. Let's do Animal Kingdom, it's the most shady and the easiest to maneuver." With mixed feelings, I responded, "Ok."

Tiffanni came into the room to wake me on the last day and to ask one last time, "Can we please go? I want to go so bad." I don't think it was about a park, or a ride- it was about independence. It was about memories. It was about being normal.

So we went. The Animal Kingdom. The place where it all started. And this time I got to feel the significance of the moment all day. Each ride, each snack, each smile from Tiffanni and our kids. We fought the heat and the extra work of a wheelchair. I noticed the beauty of the moment all day. And we smiled, and we laughed, and we played, and we were normal for one last ride.

MY FAVORITE CAMPER

I met Tiffanni at Preacher's Kids' camp. As was her MO, she was dating a jerky guy and I was intrigued. Why do great girls go for those types of guys? I found myself working for the entire weekend to make her laugh. I wanted her to escape from her dredged relationship into my light-hearted humor. She laughed a lot, but I don't know if she ever realized the contrast. She was in 9th grade, and I in 10th- 1992.

I saw her again the next year at summer camp. She said hello to me with a cautious smile, her brain churning to remember how she knew me. She tried to convince me later that she always knew it was me- embarrassed to admit I hadn't left much of an impression. But her smile was the same. It had marked me.

I met other people, but always kept my eye on her. She had a group of friends that decided they weren't going to waste time with boys that week. They spent the entire week having fun with each other. Laughing and praying together. They lingered at the altar every night crying and snotting all over each other, indifferent to anyone's opinion.

The next year I came back to camp as a graduated senior and she was a camp counselor. Stationed at the lake, making sure that us kids wore our life jackets, so I absent-mindedly forgot mine every day, just for the reprimand. Any notice was a good notice. I stood beside her and talked away the afternoons, distracting her from her life-saving- but she was doing more important work.

The next summer, I worked the camp, hoping that she would too. She didn't, but I remember one single night in two months that she showed up just to visit her friends that were there. She was taking a summer class, she told me, and couldn't come to camp that year. She sat in the camp service, in the balcony- so I did too. The best night of the summer.

That fall, she came to my college as a freshman. For the first time ever, I had her to myself. Every day I walked her to class- how else would she find her way around the campus? We ate together, went out with friends on the weekends, and I invited her to the piano practice room to sing while I played. I had just taken a beginner course and her voice made my novice chord pounding playing sound brilliant. And inevitably, I won. As all upper-classmen do, I turned on the charm and she swooned.

By the end of the school year, we were asked by one of the traveling worship teams to join. I'm certain they asked me to play piano because they knew she would be more likely to sing. With 9-months experience as a piano player, we joined a traveling representative recruiting group for our college and went to camps up and down the East Coast all summer. It was the best summer of my life. By now, you can surely tell that I have a thing for summer camps.

The next year I interned with my brother-in-law who was a youth pastor. He had recently started a summer camp called Beach Freak (which parents still furrow their brow when they hear the name.) I was asked to play piano and Tiffanni to sing. I led a small group of middle school boys (who are in their 30's now) and fell in love with the camp. After seeing and experiencing dozens of camps all over, there is nothing like it.

The next year, Tiffanni and I were married and became youth pastors. We brought our group from Tennessee to the camp and never left. That's every summer for 19 years. We've attended Beach Freak longer than every student here this year has been alive! And boy do we have the stories. We've watched teenagers find their calling, give their hearts to Christ, release the past, and embrace the future. We've seen several marriage proposals, tragedy and heartache, restoration and transformation. Beach Freak has impacted us and those we bring for two decades.

Every summer for 25 years, we've camped. I watched Tiffanni as a camper love her friends and then as a counselor, love students. Then as a youth pastor, I watched her pour her life into young people- crying and snotting every summer. I guess that's part of the experience. And then last night during the service, I watched her sit, wedged between two of our leaders so that her body couldn't flail too far to the right or left. She pinballed off of them all night. Then they escorted her to the café, arm in arm, and placed her at a picnic table to talk and laugh with everyone. Where she used to entertain, now she watched and listened. Her smile, still as bright, her eyes bounced around the table as people told their funny stories. And my favorite camper and I did what we do every summer- we hung out at camp.

THE OCEAN

My earliest vacation memory is the ocean. Everything lives in superlatives in the past, especially if you're young- bigger, stronger, longer, colder. We drove across this giant bridge in Pensacola, FL that took days to cross. I envisioned our car barreling over the rails and into the mouth of Jaws, a big thanks to my negligent parents for letting me watch that demonic horror flick in elementary school. We stayed on the bayside and built sandcastles and ate fresh seafood every night. Memories are funny that way.

Another time I was in high school and we visited the East Coast of Florida- New Smyrna Beach. A tropical storm was brewing in the Caribbean and had sent its fringe fury toward our beach. My dad stood on the shore and watched me and my two brothers body surf for hours. The waves were the largest that I had ever seen, towering above us before they crashed over and over onto us. We would position ourselves, backs to the chaos, facing the sands. As the beast would pull to swallow us whole, we would begin to swim, flailing arms, motoring feet. Timed just right, we could float to the surface of the top of the wave and let it rumble underneath. Tossing and crashing below, we could feel the uncontrolled fury just below our bellies as we tamed one wave at a time with little doubt that it could turn on us at any time and pummel us into the scattered sand.

Late last summer we were invited to some friends' house to watch the kids swim and barbeque. Tiffanni hadn't swam in over a year. I was too scared of what her body would do. It felt like another taken for granted pleasure ripped away by this disease. Dis-ease, it makes sense when you see it that way. Somehow my friend talked me into letting Tiffanni swim. "I'll swim with her and won't take my hands off of her. It'll probably cool her down." Another unforeseen consequence, because she never stops moving, she's constantly burning calories, always hot, always sweating. I acquiesced.

And something happened. Unexpected. Not just unexpected, the opposite of what I expected. Her body stilled, slowing to a rhythmic exhale and inhale, and she swam. Wrapped in a fluorescent purple noodle, she glided around the pool. Her arms motionless, her legs calm, a hushful peace buoyed her in the saltwater swimming pool. It was as if she had stumbled upon Ponce de León's healing waters. Huntington's and gravity, now reckoned powerless, traded places with Tiffanni as she regained control if only for a few moments.

For the rest of the year I anxiously awaited this summer. Was that moment an anomaly, or did water change the stars for a few moments for us?

Over the last several days we've spent some time at the beach as a family. It's ironic that the beach, which requires so much work- sunscreen, water, snacks, an umbrella, a shovel and pail, change of clothes, beach chairs, boogie board- once entered, can be so undemanding. We enter the ocean, the great equalizer of effort, and we float. Where we are all the same. Where the normal life of the past revisits us. Bobbing rhythmically with the waves, absent of tedium, in tandem with the vastness of what unites the world. The ocean. And we all swim, all of us.

ROLE REVERSAL

I don't know who thought makeup was a good idea, I don't care much for him- I'm certain it was a dumb guy named Benedict. I know what you're thinking, "Trust me, some people desperately need it." But I'm pretty sure we've just conditioned ourselves as a culture to think it's important. Kind of how each culture has a different concept of beauty. There's a group in Thailand that likes long necks, not beer, like necks. There's a tribe in Ethiopia that thinks body scars are super-sexy. America has its own self-imposed standards of beauty. Dang you Benedict.

I spent half a day at Clinique a few years ago learning how to do makeup. I have the patience and attention span of a toddler and inwardly pitched a fit as I was introduced to primers, lipstick, lip gloss, lip liner, foundation, powder, BB cream, blush, bronzer, mascara, eyeliner, eye shadow, and of course Clinique's 3-step face cleansing process- it's a racket! And concealer was invented by Satan. No wonder some women wake up with the roosters to get started. Surely long necks are easier. But, I figured it out because it mattered.

We've also spent some time with several different hair stylists trying to figure out the balance between a cool hairdo (because Tiff gets so hot), and one with some style. Not to mention, one that is easy for me to maintain. A tall order. I suggested a Sinead O'Conner, but it didn't fly. Tiffanni was a hairstylist for the few years before she was diagnosed with Huntington's. I remember the day that she graduated from hair school, we took off to Savannah in a convertible for the weekend. I had gotten tickets to a taping of the Paula Dean show because Tiff loves the Food Network and I love convertibles. I was a hero for the weekend.

I've held out on some big girl stuff for as long as I can. I think that it had something to do with not allowing my daughters to grow up too fast, because you know, girls grow up way too fast. We don't shave legs, do makeup, have cell phones, have boyfriends- stuff like that. But I finally gave in on makeup. Addyson starts 7th grade this fall and I thought we'd glide into this stuff with some powder and lipstick. Oddly enough, she didn't need much of a lesson on how to do makeup because she's been applying it for years. She learned eyeliner, powder, lipstick, blush, mascara, and eye shadow before she was 10. Addy and Carsyn share the fun with me in doing their mom's makeup. A break for me and a joy for them, at least when I let them experiment. Not always a great result.

My kids have grown up in some ways that I didn't anticipate. Tiff and I used to talk about when we would let them have certain privileges, and we always agreed, later is better. I guess we are old-fashioned that way. I can only assume that usually little girls learn to do makeup from having someone do theirs, watching someone put her makeup on, or practicing on themselves- clown cheeks and wobbly lipstick smiles included. But mine received lesson one on their mom.

Carsyn didn't understand the concept of blush at first. Layering a pink streak from lips to earlobe. But she got it. She's patient with Tiffanni's movements and talks gently to her, "Ok momma, open your eyes wide. Here comes the mascara." Addyson likes hair duty more. It seems like a limitless canvas of artistic expression. I'm waiting for the day when Tiff ends up at church with dreadlocks.

So in a not-so-surprising twist, my little girls are not so little anymore. I've protected them from every thing that I can to keep them from prematurely advancing. But I guess Time with her deep red rouge splattered cheekbones, her waterproof black mascara, and her beautifully draped and curled blowout beckons my babies onward. There's no stopping her- not only does she stop for no one, but she expects to be all dolled up in the process.

A CHANGE IN HER GAIT

Monday was our fifth anniversary. We've gone to the same place every year- same routine, same time, same smells, same faces. I remember the first visit in 2011 most vividly. Not simply because it was the first time, but because it was different. It's like going to Disney World every year for a decade. The only one that you remember is the one that it rains all day, or your brother gets kicked off of a ride for trying to punch Goofy's nose off, or you get chosen as the crowd representative for a highlight show- you remember that. I also remember this past Monday pretty well- those four visits in between, however, all run together.

That first visit was surreal. That's how I remember it. The Doctor looked at Tiffanni and within five minutes made his diagnosis. Five minutes. I could hear it in his voice from the second that he shook her hand. "Squeeze," he said. "Hmm." The difference between a "Hmph" and a "Hmm" is all in the tone. "Hmph" has a distasteful snide sound to it, but "Hmm" carries an inevitability that is easy to recognize if you're listening for it. I'm sure that my subconscious knew what he would say, I mean you can't watch the changes for a year and not take note, but I was shocked all the same.

"Uh oh, I hear the change in your gait," we were greeted with as we made our way down the hall for the sixth time. Hmph. So that's all that represents the last year of our lives? The change in her gait. We sat in the same two chairs across the same desk in front of the same doctor. His back to four bookshelves of medical journals, family pictures, med school textbooks, and a candle. There was plenty of time to appraise the contents of the sterile shelves while he skimmed through five years worth of scribbled notes to himself. I sat there readjusting my posture every few seconds, wondering if he had a made a note of her gait from last year.

The summation of the last year of our lives is the size of Tiffanni's gait. A smaller, wobbly, slower step, she leans against me more now, especially going up stairs. He has no idea how I've fought getting a wheelchair all year. We went to Six Flags at the end of last summer and took a wheelchair. My kids cried to themselves when they saw her in it for the first time. I could have done better preparing them, but what do you say? It's less about what to declare and more about how to answer when the questions come. So, I've fought it. Once you sit in a wheelchair, you never get out of it again. Ever.

Her stride. She uses it to stumble down sloped aisles to take her place in church now. She lays sprawled out in an entire pew, just me and her, sometimes her and my parents or her parents. Right in front of the side of the stage where she used to sing. Last fall I found a cassette tape of her and her best friend Candy singing with her music minister Ben. They recorded a full album of worship songs out in Texas in the early 90's. I came across a box of them packing for our move, a whole box, and pulled out three before I tossed the rest out.

They were stocking stuffers for Addy, Car, and Brayden this Christmas. "Your mom used to be the greatest singer. I thought you'd want to hear her and somehow unearthed these while we were packing!" Santa came through.

Her traipse. It's the closest thing to a skip in her step that I can find when I'm taking her to get into a pool. She loves the pool. We discovered it this year, the only thing that calms her and stills her body. She sweats through every month, burns through every calorie, including the 1100 calorie peanut butter milkshake that my mom makes for her every afternoon as a "snack." It was our quick fix when we couldn't keep up with her weight-loss this winter. At best we've stabilized it. She can't eat enough food to compensate for the energy that she burns as she moves erratically all day. Lying, sitting, standing, there's no reprieve anymore. And then we found the water. She now asks to swim everyday, so we load up the car as often as we can and find a pool, lake, creek, ocean. Anything for a reprieve.

So much taken, not a lot given. Yes. It's been a full year of change. Not just for her, but for the kids, and me, and my parents, and her parents, and everyone that is around her. This, at times, mindnumbingly slow lumber, and at other times, barreling gallop has been anything but stagnation.

So yeah, Doc. There seems to have been a change in her gait. We'll see you next year.

CHRISTMAS IN JULY

I sat around a craft table filled with my other 7 year old classmates. I vividly remember sitting around that crayon crusted table with Krista and Kenneth- mostly because Kenneth and I were vying for Krista's affection. "I don't believe in Santa Clause, do you?" Krista announced with an arrogant authority. If my mom and I wouldn't have already had that talk, I would have never admitted it. It's funny what you remember after more than 30 years. I was seven.

A couple of nights ago we sat around the dinner table. Brayden, without provocation asked, "Dad, tell me if you're Santa Clause." I've gotten pretty good over almost 20 years of youth ministry in not reacting to what people declare- you hear a lot. You can shut a teenager down in seconds with a furrowed brow.

"Where did this come from?" I deflected.

"Dad, are you Santa Clause? And I need to know about the Easter Bunny too." My face had to alter. This is my last believer. My last dreamer.

"Buddy, don't you want there to be a Santa Clause? I sure do?"

"I want the truth," he demanded, his eager eyes boring a hole into my soul. My little Tom Cruise.

I fired back, "You can't handle the truth! You don't want the truth because deep down in places you don't talk about at parties, you want me on that wall, you need me on that wall." Ok, I didn't say that, but have I written about how much I love Aaron Sorkin?

"Buddy, I want there to be a Santa Clause. You don't want it to be me, do you?" I said as I grasped for another ever-fraying strand to a former life. And with that, we moved on.

Later that night, upstairs in his room/guest room/play room/music room/where I hide to nap (third kid, tough luck) room, we sat on the couch playing guitar together. He's learned seven chords in seven days and somewhere between D and A minor he stopped. "Is mom gonna die?" He stared at me with the same truth needy eyes. And he grew up. Just like that. You always hear how kids grow up in a flash, right before your eyes. But this lightning struck too precisely, too directly.

The girls have asked the same question and I've never had a good answer. Years to prepare, seconds to avoid. "I mean, we're all going to die." "No, of course not." "Well, it's complicated." "You know, we're going to keep praying and keep loving her no matter what." "Look at me, I'm going to take care of your mom- don't worry about her or me." "They're doing amazing Huntington's research right now. I bet we'll have a cure before long."

So, I rifled through my bag of responses, situated somewhere between frets and strings, naiveté and candor, and shot something back to divert. Not because he doesn't deserve an answer. And not even because he's not ready for something. But because I'm not. And I taught him another chord. Anything to keep Santa alive.

IT'S THE LITTLE THINGS

There are a lot of big things to be thankful for. My parents, my family, my church, my friendships. And I'm sure that I overlook them and take them for granted sometimes- not as often as I would have thought. If this disease does anything, it slows me down and helps me to reflect. But every once in a while, a thought will hit, and I'll think, "I sure am lucky for that."

I was late to puberty (by today's standards). A girl once asked me in 7th grade why I didn't have any hair on my legs. On the spot, "I shave them. I'm a knife collector and that's how you tell if your knife is sharp." Brilliant. I've had better days. Tiffanni lost motor skills before we had time to plan. About a year into helping her do everything it occurred to me, I haven't shaved her legs. I panicked and began to think through all of my options- shaving, waxing, sharpening my non-existent knife collection, laser (is that a thing?), removing her legs altogether. And then I looked- she has no leg hair. Like none. Whether it was the disease, the medicine, or genetics, I hit the jackpot. Lucky her, she gets to keep her legs. It's the little things.

She and I go to Dairy Queen and a movie every Friday. We'll

see about 45 movies this year. A lot of them are good, some of them not so much (I'm looking at you *Divergent: Allegiant*), all of them an escape. But something that never fails- Dairy Queen. If you'll just lower your expectations a little, the burger and fries and a blizzard are spot on. I had a kidney stone last year and gave up soft drinks, but on Fridays- I splurge. Root Beer is my guilty pleasure. But when it's time to go, I have to figure out a way to leave with two drinks and Tiffanni. That's a three handed problem. She gets one hand and lucky for me, my other hand is the perfect size to hold two drinks. Whether it's big hands or small cups, it works. Tiff in the right and Dairy Queen in the left. There's not a Friday that goes by that I don't think about that perfect combination. It's the little things.

I was never a curser, but if there's anything in the universe that is damned by God, it's disease. To listen in on a cathartic explosion of shared frustration once in a while opens a relief valve, if only for a moment. I'm grateful for friends who grieve with me. They bargain, and cry, and deal, and curse the things that are cursed in my life. One of my closest friends fills in the gaps when I can't. Where I don't have the space for anger or to feel for that matter- he lets somebody have it. I'm not exactly sure who Somebody is, but that person would be so offended if they heard him. So that no one ever gets too vaunted of an image of me- I like when someone curses for me and more importantly, for Tiffanni, out of a desperation for justice. Tiffanni is proof that bad things happen to good people. And sometimes safe words don't express this violation. It's the little things.

Over and over I've noticed the serendipity of the timing of this disease. If it was going to happen- there are some things that make it better now. The big things are my parents in a place where they could uproot their lives and build a house with me. And my church that affords me the pleasure of doing what I love and the space to take care of the ones that I love. The other day, Tiffanni and I were at the movie theater and I've noticed the last few times she's struggled to go to the bathroom by herself. She usually takes about 15 minutes- just long enough for me to start evaluating women to see who I could ask to check on her. But she always stumbles out. So a few movies ago, I went to the General Manager and told him our situation. He said that he sees us every Friday. I asked him, "If there is anyway possible that remodeling is on the agenda in the future, would you consider a family bathroom?" He skirted the request with the legalities, and bringing everything up to code, and such. But then said to me, "You know what, take her in there with you. I don't mind and no one around here will mind. Lastly, because of the last few months, no one can really say anything anyway." And with that, we resurrected movies. They're ours for as long as we want them and nothing really stops us. So, the angry people can have their boycotts and feigned outrage. I'm going to take Tiffanni to the bathroom. Without it, we lose movies, and movies are important. And in this case, timing is important. It's the little things.

It's not all bad. And I'm not just spinning this thing. Because there are so many parts of our life that are tragic. But there are bright spots, suspiciously providential spots, that float around our lives everyday waiting to be noticed. And enough little things make this big thing a little more bearable.

VILLAGE PEOPLE

Four inches. That's one inch for each season over the last twelve months- Fall, Winter, Spring, and finally Summer. He was devastated when he stood under the green mark at Goliath last year and it was obvious that he was two inches short- and that was with his tall shoes on. "Sorry, you're not quite there yet champ." I could sense the disdain that Brayden collected in his heart for each of the teenage gatekeepers doing their jobs. But not this year. Four inches in a year catapulted him into the Ride-It-All Group. So he did.

Six Flags has made its way into tradition with my crew. We've gone every summer for several years now and the kids look forward to it. Tiff starts asking about it by October. They count down the days and catalog the rides by name. I had to tell the girls last year to take it easy talking about the attractions that Brayden couldn't ride because he wasn't tall enough yet. Goliath, Batman, Superman, DareDevil- every young boy's dream. I also had to tell them to stop talking about the Teacups, you know, the one he was plenty tall enough to ride. Why couldn't it just be named Deathtrap or Tilt-a-Torture. Something that would allow him to keep his man card.

We spend a bazillion dollars every June to spend a single day at Disney, the Happiest Place on Earth, and all the kids talk about all year is Six Flags. They're practically giving away tickets. The kids' school gave them free tickets for reading books throughout the last school year. Reading books. Isn't that like a requirement at school? And then Tiffanni and I got half-priced tickets just for breathing.

But Six Flags is hard. Whoever laid it out apparently worked for the US Government's Health Initiative. There are no flat areas, it's all peaks and valleys, summits and fjords. Which is hard enough walking all day in the blazing asphalt desert heat, but we've got a wheelchair. I hate it, but it's wheelchair or nothing. Tiffanni's balance is worse than ever so it's her only reprieve. Now I'm an eternal optimist, but I don't know how to stay positive with three young children, a disabled wife, a wheelchair, and a day in the Sahara. So I call in the big guns. My brother and sister and their spouses.

My greatest fear throughout the process of this disease is that my kids would miss out on something. And then missing out on something would scar them or inhibit them. Doing double duty on "Dad, watch this," and "Guess what we did today," and "Dad, we need to talk," is a job for two loving parents. There's this brilliant design where parents nurture their kids' dreams and talents and personalities and the kids have the greatest shot at health and stability. But sometimes it just doesn't work out. It rocks me some days. I just can't do it. I'm sure there are super hero single parents out there that fill all of the gaps, but I'm not that. Far from it.

So I don't. I don't fill all of the gaps. I don't even fill most of them. Because the greatest gift that I have ever received are the gap fillers in my life. The cookers and cleaners, attention givers and school shoe buyers, dream nurturers and problem listeners, clothes shoppers and dessert makers, grass cutters and clothes washers, meal preparers and cart-the-kids-all-over-the-world drivers, ball game watchers and house builders, pastors and Sunday School teachers, "just because" gift givers and school project helpers, hair cutters and braid tie-ers, sports coaches and swim lesson givers, and Six Flags kid ride partners and wheelchair pushers. It takes a village to raise kids with health and stability. Where they don't miss out on anything even though they're missing out on so much. It takes a village to fill all of the gaps and make sure that kids never doubt that they are loved deeply and cherished daily.

So when my family needed a village, they got the best. This is my village. And these are my people.

THE TRADEOFF

There was a time that I could sleep until 2pm in the afternoon. No breaks, no getting up to let the dog out, no Mother Nature reprieves- just sleep. I would stay up until 1am or 2am and crash. Twelve, thirteen hours of siesta and just because I enjoyed myself so much, sometimes I would take a nap later. In my college apartment, my roommates and I fitted the windows with aluminum foil and blacked out our room. A bomb shelter where nothing got in or out. Not that sunlight was issue for me, we tricked our brains into thinking it was always time to sleep. That's what you do when you stay up all night playing ping-pong and need to nap for a few hours during a class break.

Nights have gotten hard lately. Sleep is a commodity. Huntington's affects movement, cognition, and mood. For over four years I never saw much of an effect on Tiffanni's mood. She was happy, content, even carefree- especially to carry so much. But lately, her anxiety is getting the better of her. Household items are out of place. She needs Tylenol. Her hair needs to be brushed again. She's hungry. She's tired. She can't sleep. She won't sit down. The kids are too loud. The kids are in the house. We have kids. And for a while now, her seemingly incessant worry has creeped into our house sanity. It can be especially tough when I'm not home sometimes. Who knew that I could have a calming effect?

So I called her Doctor and told him that something had to give. She had to sleep. I had to sleep. So he prescribed Ambien. Tiff used to sleepwalk and talk in her sleep. One time I caught her digging through a potato bag at the bottom of the pantry. "What are you doing?" I asked, arrested from a REM cycle after hearing the cabinets banging in the kitchen.

"I'm looking for my pants," she said. The look that followed inferred, what else do you think that I would be doing?

Another time she woke me up in a panic with an AK-47 cadence of nudges to my kidney. "Someone is in our shower!" When I came to my bearings, I thought to myself that that was impossible.

"No one is in the shower Tiff, you're asleep." But it's hard to reason with someone and convince them that they are asleep when they're carrying on a conversation with you.

"I thought you were the man," she responded. Not the man, I had never claimed that (except when bragging about my unbeaten Monopoly streak.) The man. So I got up to check the shower. I slung back the shower curtain, fist cocked, just in case the .1% chance that someone was in there, I was prepared.

"See," I said, "There's no one in there just like I told you." I glared at her, only to hear her snoring again.

But Ambien was another thing altogether. Not only did she

not sleep, she got up and did chores. I caught her sprawled out like Cinderella cleaning out the bathroom vanity one night. Brushing her hair for over an hour another. And the whole time talking to me. If I wouldn't respond, she would nudge me over and over again. I retreated to the couch several times, but she would go wake the kids. So I called the Doctor again. This time he prescribed something different.

And she slept.

But, there was a tradeoff. Her response time slowed. Her ability to reason and converse changed. Her balance regressed to early childhood. Her fine motor skills lessened.

But she slept.

They don't give you a playbook on the household health quotient. My sanity and her incoherence vs. my insanity and her sense of reality, her anxiety. If I just knew the right thing to do, I would do it. If someone said, "On Monday, just grin and bear it and let her breathe. But on Tuesday, medicate her so you can catch up on sleep." That would be simple. But there's no way to calculate the cost of stress in a home. Not on her, not on us. There's no textbook that offers an equation to solve for health. So, we wing it. I fly blind. I guess and pray that it's the right thing.

I've been married to the same woman for almost eighteen years, but she's not the same woman. I don't think that I expected that she would be. But who knows what you expect when you're a the-world-is-my-oyster kid. And it's not like the vows promised that nothing would change- quite the opposite actually. There's a sense of contentment with the trajectory and growth for one of us. A sense of loss and sadness for the decline of the other. And it frustrates me that they might be inextricably connected. Some tradeoffs are good. Some, not so much. I just wish that I could discern the difference.

HOLY SATURDAY

Saturday mornings are for sleeping in. They're for lazy traipses into the living room only to plop back down on the couch and submit to the weight of your eyelids once again for a mid-morning nap. They are for brunch. Not breakfast because that would require cooking and eating too early which is blasphemy to a snoozy Saturday morning.

But this past Saturday morning something encroached on my well-planned unplanned day. Addyson is a cheerleader and her squad was invited to cheer at a special needs sports program's opening day. So us early birds rushed down the interstate 30 minutes south, sans breakfast (to buy an extra few minutes of sleep) at dawn so that we could beat the sweltering August heat.

We arrived to a bustle of activity. Moms and dads, brothers and sisters, coaches and guardians aiding in the ready-making of their loved one. The opening day ceremony field was littered with wheelchairs, walkers, canes, and arm braces. Children stumbled around the field in an unorganized commotion as their coaches tried to coax them into standing still for the pomp and circumstance. Good luck with that.

The stands were full of eager and nervous fans when out walked, to my surprise, the voice of the Alabama Crimson Tide- Eli Gold. The voice that had called half a dozen national championships, colored the games of the gods as he commentated arguably the greatest college football program in the history of the sport, stood at the center of the field and helped tie a few shoes. When he spoke I assumed that it would feel misplaced. His usual Saturdays spent with super-humans, this day he would paint the play of the powerless.

With the opening pitch thrown, the games began. The coaches and helpers and cheerleaders numbered a 1:1 ratio to the players. The competitive fury of a normal sports day was replaced with patience and gentle voices. The stands felt the same as the crowd roared for every foul tip, every bunt stretched into a triple, every in-the-park, in-the-infield homerun.

The next day churches would fill with millions of men, women, and children in their Sunday best, but they would be hard pressed to find a more holy place than this sweltering August Saturday morning ball field.

There's something sacred about a group of people who sacrifice their time and effort for a group of unnoticed children. Those who bring value to the unvalued by noticing the unnoticed. Where longsuffering replaces the fever of competition and the unabled bodied take center stage. The sanctity of that space is unmatched by any ornate stained glass cathedral.

Tiffanni doesn't offer the same energy and life to every room that she once did. For the first time that I've known her, she fades into the corners- my wallflower. Her conversations are labored, her attention wains. But more times than not, when we're out, when we're at church, when we visit a friend, someone gets down on a knee, looks eye to eye with her and focuses all of their attention into her face. She's slow to respond, a tardy grin on her best days. She can't initiate, can't reciprocate in the way that she once did.

But I notice.

I notice the patient one-sided conversations from a friend. I see the hand holds, cheek kisses, arm rubs, neck massages, minutes spent fanning the heat away. Each moment of value to the unvalued doesn't escape me. I have never been a great giver or receiver of gifts, but there is none greater than the attention given my bride. So, to you who care so much and have noticed- thank you. If there are jewels or crowns or robes or mansions in the next life, and if I somehow wind up with something- you noticers can have mine. But I doubt it will come to that, for in my understanding of the Supreme, you've earned the greatest reward heaven bestows.

WORDS

I was a pretty good kid. My greatest fault was my mouth. Not the shape, arguably, but the use. I just couldn't keep it shut. There was something percolating on the inside at all times and it just had to get out. Words. And they always bid farewell to my mouth at the worst possible times. You know how most people think something, but there's this tactful voice on the inside that says, "Now's not the time for that." Yeah, my voice on the inside had laryngitis.

However, over the years I've mellowed. There aren't as many things up there rapping on the door to get out. Still plenty, but not as desperate to be heard. I'm sure some of my friends would argue, but they wouldn't have known me as a kid. I had to be heard. I read once that we all mature into introversion. Some of us just have a longer journey. A Pilgrim's Progress.

A study came out a couple of years ago that said that women had a larger amount of Foxp2 protein in their systems. This protein has a connection to chattiness. According to the survey, women speak on average around 20,000 words per day while men speak closer to 7,000. Maybe I had some extra Foxp2 laying around unused when I was younger, but it's not there anymore. It was handed down through heredity to my two daughters. Every ounce.

They talk.

Like, they talk a lot.

I'm quite certain that they've been mainlining Foxp2 for years. Addicts.

Addyson talks about details. She came to me the other day and asked, "Dad, do you want to hear what kind of cake that I have planned for your birthday?" I looked up from my book as she anticipated a yes from my eyes I suppose. "It's going to be a three layer cake. I'm thinking red velvet which is your favorite. Do you want butter cream or cream cheese icing?" I think I blinked. "Cream cheese of course. No one eats butter cream with red velvet." Then she began to describe the design. I would tell you about it if I didn't check out around the types of icing tips that she would use for the bottom of the first layer. I woke her up a few mornings ago and she opened her eyes and said, "Wanna hear about my dream? I was in an alternate universe…" And we were off. No warm up, no prep, just go. She talks cake design, party favors, dreams, cheer routines, types of formations, musicians, friends' drama, books- she doesn't know what a synopsis is, *Dance Moms*, clothes, shopping, movies (and through movies- she commentates because who wanted to hear the actors anyways), you name it- she uses her words.

Carsyn uses her words in a different way. She's inquisitive and thoughtful. Easy answers don't suffice. Fairness is the Golden Rule. It won't be long until she puts God on the witness stand and has Him answer for the injustices of the world. We had a crazy conversation the other night. "Some kids called me and the other girls lesbians today at school and it upset me."

"Why?"

"Because they meant it ugly and it hurt my feelings."

"Are you?" I asked.

"A lesbian? No."

"Then why do you care? You know the truth so why does it matter?"

"Because it hurt my feelings."

Then I tried to use dad logic. Not worthwhile most of the time with Addyson, she needs to be felt, but Carsyn processes differently. "It's kind of like if someone called you a mean racial slur. Would that hurt your feelings?"

And my 11 year old out logic-ed me. "No dad. You see, I'm not black or Hispanic or Asian and will never be. I can't be. I can't change into something that I'm not. So that wouldn't hurt. But I could be gay- it's possible. And so could one of my friends. So, it hurt my feelings."

And that's our conversations. Deep thoughts from an eleven year old. Questions about her mom. About the possibility of the future and her career. Her college. Scholarships. Marriage. Children. Fears. Joys. She uses her words.

There are these words that have to come out. They are

tempered by personality and experience. And I have to work hard to hear all of them. It's obvious that I don't use as many as they do, but I also have a hard time hearing as many as they use. But I focus until I go cross-eyed sometimes. A half dozen classes in counseling and psychology didn't prepare me for this. And I wasn't born with the gift of listening like their mom was. She could feel and empathize with every emotion. She could infer what wasn't there and intuit what was before it was even said. You could see it in her eyes. She laughed when someone laughed and could release a tear as soon as the person across from her began to weep. She would have won a gold medal in synchronized crying. She would have laid in bed with the girls for hours talking about life, listening to middle school gossip, and stifling drama. We would have rarely used the radio on road trips. Every family fun game night would have been hijacked by conversation, which is probably the point anyway. And she and I would have partnered to be the best hearers ever. If I'd only known that she would lose her words so soon I would have listened more, concentrated harder, focused better. I would have filed some of them away in a drawer for a rainy day. Shoulda, coulda, woulda. Today, I just miss her words.

RUN FORREST RUN

When Tiffanni was diagnosed with Huntingtons almost five years ago, it didn't shock me. It wasn't a relief in the way that when something is wrong it's nice to have an idea of what is wrong. It was a relief in that we could blame something for a couple of job losses, her new clumsiness, and some erratic behavior.

I don't remember shock. It might have been because I knew what the doctor would say long before we scheduled the appointment. Or it might have been shock masked in indifference. The human body is brilliant in that it usually does what it needs to do to communicate changes that need to happen. All of us have headaches. The body gives us that to tell us to do something. Unfortunately, we usually do the wrong thing- take Tylenol. The problem is that it's not like we have an acetaminophen deficiency. It's because we're dehydrated, or tired, or stressed, or overworked, or need glasses. So when the body shuts down to life-changing news with no response- it's saying something.

Most people have heard of the stages of grief. DABDA.

Denial, anger, bargaining, depression, acceptance. I wish they were that clean and orderly. It would be easy to see a season of denial and tell yourself, "Be ready, soon you're going to go through a season of anger. You're not going to know why you're irritated at the world, but it's part of the process." That would be nice. But it just doesn't work that way.

It would also be nice if the stages acted the way that you think that they should. Most think that denial means this nonacceptance of the facts of loss. "No, he's not dead." "No, you're lying to me, that didn't happen." And it certainly comes out that way once in awhile. But it usually shows up in a different way. The most common way is that denial shows up by making a person believe that their loss hasn't affected them as deeply as it really has. "I just have to be strong for my family right now." "I thought it would be very hard, but it hasn't affected me as much as I thought it would." All crap.

I was super lucky. I was in a doctoral program when I found out about Tiff that required me to meet with two different counselors- not because of the diagnosis, it was part of the program. Those meetings changed everything for me. I remember my first meeting ever. I thought that I was different, that I was handling my situation inappropriately. I was very nervous to admit some of my thoughts. I kept playing this whole scenario out in my head, all the way to the end. And I just knew that that was wrong. And for some reason I told my counselor. Ready for a chastisement, "Jeremy, you can't do that. You have to take things as they come," or something like that. And instead he looked at me and nonchalantly said, "Well of course you do. That's what everyone does. In fact, if you didn't play all of it out, we'd have to talk about some more serious stuff. You're in an okay place." And with those few words, the trajectory of my health, self-grace, and coping changed forever.

One of the first things that I learned in professional counseling was that I had to exercise. My body needed endorphins and hormones and such to be firing in order to balance the depression that would inevitably come. You did see the DABDA, right? Good luck avoiding one of those stages. So I exercised. I tried all kinds of things. Tennis, mountain biking, weights, swimming, and most recently running. I've run off and on for almost a year.

A few months ago I decided to set a goal. A triathlon. Who knows why. My dad said that 40 year olds feel the fleeting passing of youth and so they try to hold on to it. Thanks Dad. I'll be 40 in a few months. Sayonara youth. My triathlon is in October. Mostly so that I can still land in the 35-39 age bracket. Ironically, the 40's age bracket is more competitive. But I didn't know what to expect. I don't know what to expect. I've never raced anything in my life that I needed to train for. So, to give myself a little litmus test and to see whether I would be ready in October, I ran my first 10K this weekend.

It was hot, humid, hilly, and hellacious. The night before I got nervous and googled "first race tips." The Google told me to "Fight through the pain" and "Have a mantra." I'm a pretty simple man, so my mantra was, "Fight through the pain." And when I started mile 2, I started saying it. And I repeated it for the next five miles. After about 5,000 repetitions, I finished it. The mantra and the race.

So I ran. While running doesn't change my situation, it changes my perspective of it. And at least for today, it keeps me from running away from my situation. It helps me to stay healthy physically, emotionally, and mentally. So, if you see me out early in the morning running, please don't run over me with your car. That wouldn't help very much.

"That day, for no particular reason, I decided to go for a little run. So I ran to the end of the road. And when I got there, I thought maybe I'd run to the end of town. And when I got there, I thought maybe I'd just run across Greenbow County. An• I figure•, since I'• run this far, maybe I'd just run across the great state of Alabama. And that's what I did. I ran clear across Alabama. For no particular reason I just kept on going. I ran clear to the ocean. An• when I got there, I figure•, since I'd gone this far, I might as well turn around, just keep on going. When I got to another ocean, I figure•, since I'• gone this far, I might as well just turn back, keep right on going."

A LABORED DAY

Holidays are hard. Not the big ones. You can fake your way through those. The small ones. That's where the holes are glaring. With Christmas and Thanksgiving, family comes over. We sit around and eat ham, turkey, potato casserole, green beans, you know- the healthier stuff that I'm willing to list. Of course, I could have written how we always have as many sweets as we do healthy food (which by the way is a loose term in the South- it just means not sweet.) And to be completely honest, I'm including sweet potato casserole and strawberry pretzel salad in the healthy sides because they have some healthy words associated with them- potato and salad. Good enough for me.

We eat and laugh and yell at the kids to close the door as they come lumbering in and out a million times, covered in nature and pied pipering the state's cartel of horseflies. The adults usually group up and go shopping or to the movies. Guess which group I make. Vacation fits in with the big holidays too. Because there's an agenda, a purpose. You know where you're going and what you're doing. And if you don't, you'll figure it out because you're somewhere new and normal rules don't apply. You don't have to be as thrifty, no bedtimes, no food rules (as if above made you think we're strict food rule people).

But these in-between holidays are hard. Long weekend holidays. Labor day and Memorial Day and Veterans Day and MLK Day and such. There's an expectation from my kids to do something fantastic since they're out of school. Out of school means adventure. All I can think of is the complications that come with performing and pleasing when I just want to lay on the couch and take naps. Like multiple naps. I would just take one full-day long nap, but I usually get woken up by a full-mouthed decibel destroying kid or a slimy tongued dog lick to the face. So naps. Plural.

There's this pressure that I feel on the inside that life is flying by so fast and I have to make memories. I already have two of my three kids in middle school! And I dread the thought of my kids having this memory of Dad sleeping through the adventure. I envision us sitting around the dinner table years from now, me nodding off as I hear one of them say, "Remember how we learned to tip toe across the crackling hardwood floor so we wouldn't wake dad up while he took one of his holiday-sleep-life-away-rip-van-winkle-lost-opportunity-all-day slumbers?"

"Yeah, dad is the heaviest sleeper. Remember how he slept through our childhoods?" One would say through a diluted grin. And I would awaken to all of them staring and laughing at me. I would laugh along with them so that we could all pretend like it didn't matter, but deep down, I would sense the resentment and regret from them.

You know, that's what the evil mind will do- play out the whole thing to its worst possible conclusion.

That's what small holidays do. There's a simple rhythm of a normal day to the routine of school, sports practices, dinner, homework, and bedtime prayers. No pressure because there's no room for memories. No one remembers every common dinner or monotonous history report. But those danged short holidays. They scream at me, "Do something! Rent a hot air balloon. Go canoeing. Go deep sea fishing. Take them paint balling, mountain bike riding. Search for hidden treasure, make a movie, build a fort, climb a mountain, go rustle some cattle. Do something! Do anything but nap. Rest is for the weak, those who don't care about memories."

So we float through the big holidays. They come and go and just are. They're simple and easy and then they're gone. We make happy memories and live traditions and look forward to the next year where we get to do it again, mindless, but far from meaningless. But a small holiday makes me aware of an emptiness that echoes when it's over. Like an ache or a reminder that it wasn't whole. That if things were different, then things would be different. That it wasn't enough. A missed opportunity. A lost possibility. A Labored Day.

BEHIND THE MUSIC

I grew up during a transitional time for church worship music. We had a small youth group and my best friend Joe would make a mix tape of gospel songs for us to sing at the beginning of our youth meeting. His mom was a packrat and had a slide projector laying around, so Joe and I would make slides to throw the words on the wall because we thought the overhead projector was too archaic and we wanted to be cutting edge. He could change from "Jehovah Jireh" to "Spring Up A Well" with the touch of a button. Techies.

During my junior year the music minister bought a set of drums for the church and asked me if I would be our drummer. I played the trumpet in middle school, so it only made sense. I spent the next two years boom chucking for the adult service. My friend Joe, who was proficient at the piano decided that we could get rid of the mix tape in youth and go live. So we formed a band. We were the Black Keys before there was a Black Keys.

When I left for Bible College I told myself that I would learn the piano because when I became a youth minister, I didn't want to have to go back to mix tapes. At least we would have one instrument. So my freshman year of school, I took a keyboarding class where I learned chords. I then got a private tutor who actually played and toured with Prince for the last several years. I feel like I should be better. He worked with me for about a year.

On campus there was a small building between the guys and girls dorms that had been converted into a hallway of individual piano rooms. When Tiff and I started dating, she would go in there with me and I would have her sing along while I played. At some point, she talked me into singing with her. I had never sung in my life in a way that I intended on people enjoying. She heard me sing and said, "You're amazing!" I didn't believe her, but the more I sang with her, the better I thought that I sounded. She kept telling me how good I sounded and I kept singing. At some point, I think that I actually starting believing her. Not that I was amazing, but that I could at least carry the tune. During my junior year of college, we were asked to come lead worship at a church service with my friend Andy. I was extremely nervous, but Tiff kept telling me that I could do it. We arrived at the location early so I could get a feel for the out of tune piano and I led my first worship service ever to a Nursing Home filled with elderly people who kept screaming at us to, "Sing louder, I can't hear you."

When it came time to interview for our first youth ministry job, Tiff told me to write on my resumé that I could lead worship too. There were more opportunities for those that had both abilities. Somehow I just believed her that I could do it. My second time to ever lead worship was for an interview in Tennessee. For some reason, they hired us. And I just kept believing Tiffanni that I could do it. She made me sound so much better than I was and made me believe that I could actually sing. I got better at piano, picked up the guitar, and started playing it too. And she just kept telling me how good I was. Believing music into me. Music that without her, would have never been discovered.

I drove back from Nashville last night thinking about the journey from mix-tape-slide-projector-button-pusher, to hack drummer, to Nursing Home worship leader, to today. I had just finished recording my third album with my friend Sean in his studio. I shocked him when I told him that he and I had written, played, and recorded over forty songs together in the last four years. Each one of them, a single person's belief in me away from ever being created.

Creating music has become therapeutic for me. The process of sitting at a piano, experimenting with chords and melodies, tones and lyrics, cathartic. The greatest pain of my life and the therapy by which I deal with it, stem from the same person. The pleasure and pain of music, another paradox in my life, were brought to me unintentionally by the same person. While we sat in those make shift piano rooms in the mid-90's, I don't think Tiffanni ever saw me writing and recording songs in Nashville. But without her words of belief after each missed note sung and each wrong chord played, I would never have written one. And four and a half years ago, I took my first trip to Nashville searching for a way to deal with her diagnosis. It's ironic to me that she gave me a way out, a way to deal with our future. The future that she had no idea that we would have.

So, on November 1st of this year, my 40th birthday, I'll release my second studio album with a live concert CD release party. The songs about life, love, pain, heartache, joy, pleasure, grief, and hope- most of the emotions that I had never felt that first time in the piano room when she told me, "You can really sing. I promise. Why would I lie?" I'll look out into the crowd of people and see her smiling at me, mostly unaware of what any of the songs are about, listening proudly without a clue that we're all in that room, listening to that music, because of her. The reason behind the songs, the reason for the songs, and the reason they ever had the ability to come to life.

THE PASTOR

I love being a pastor. But there are days that I don't want to be a pastor anymore. Soulwork is hard work. Raising a family is hard work. Lives and marriages and young people and God's dream for their lives weigh heavy some days. And my life is already heavy some days. The days that my life is light and pastoring is heavy are manageable and the days that pastoring is light and my life is heavy are manageable, but it's those doubled-up, when it rains it pours days that get me.

The day that Carsyn cries because she doesn't want to go shopping with anyone but Tiffanni for private things and someone leaves the church because, well, who knows, because they didn't tell anyone- those days are a lot.

And the day that Tiffanni's medicine doesn't cooperate and she calls me a dozen times to ask the same question and to tell me that there are ants in the house everywhere, yet no one else sees them and I find out that a couple in the church is getting a divorce- those days are a lot.

And the days that I didn't sleep the night before because one of the kids is sick and I don't have anyone to split parent duty with while I clean sheets and floors, and give medicine every 4 hours, and check temps and hold back hair over a toilet and I have to preach a sermon that refuses to come out with any clarity because all of the clarity was spent on sanity- those days are a lot.

When heavy days outnumber light days, God's voice and assurance gets lost in the weight.

About a year after Tiffanni was diagnosed, the adrenaline rush of "I can do this" had worn off, I didn't want to pastor anymore. Everything was too much. I began to think through other options, those options where I could support my family and leave work at the office. Check out when I wasn't at work. I don't think I've ever heard God speak to my heart the way that He did in that season. One day in prayer, or maybe it wasn't prayer since it was an overwhelmed season. Maybe I was making school lunches or something menial, which makes much more sense. I felt like I heard God impress upon me,

"Jeremy, the church needs you. I want you to give her the grace and the space to live a difficult life with a certainty that I won't leave. I need you to speak honestly and authentically about how you feel. That you have doubts about faith, and church, and healing, and me. And those doubts can't sabotage faith or dead end hope. The church, especially the Pentecostal church, needs to hear about grief and loss. They need to stop pretending that things will get better because they believe it hard enough. That I am a healer and I am a sustainer, and sometimes only one at a time. But never simply because they want me to be badly enough. I need your voice, your posture, your failure, and your hope."

And then I heard,

"Jeremy, you need the church. I'm not coming to live with you, to help you, to defend you, to uplift you, to heal you- that's the job of my church. And if you don't let the church do that, then you've left me no options. My church is strong and resilient. She functions best when she realizes a clear mission and you and your family are part of that. Let me love you and take care of you through my church. I have given you to the church, now let me give the church to you. She will be my hands and heart. She will love you the way that I love you."

And with that, I rededicated my life to the church. Heavy days and light days. I have seen her at her best. The way that she has loved me and my family is the strength of my faith. I have felt, sensed, and experienced a tangible Jesus because she has shared my burden.

I love being a pastor. God saved me and asked me to be a pastor, and he saved me by allowing me to be a pastor, and he saves me while I pastor. I love His body and His body loves me and Jesus loves me inside of this beautiful, mysterious give and take. This I know.

"I am a pastor. My work has to do with God and souls— immense mysteries that no one has ever seen at any time. But I carry out this work in conditions—place and time—that I see and measure wherever I find myself, whatever time it is. There is no avoiding the conditions. I want to be mindful of the conditions. I want to be as mindful of the conditions as I am of the holy mysteries." - Eugene Peterson

ROCKABYE BABY

We brought Addyson home from the hospital after spending one night in the NICU and one night in a regular room. She was jaundiced and had to sleep in a bilirubin bed that would send light to her body throughout the day. I laid the entire bed onto our Queen-sized bed with Tiffanni, "There's no way that she's not sleeping with me." And I slept on a couch that I pulled into the bedroom and sandwiched between our bed and a wall. She and Tiffanni glowed all night long and slept like the world only existed in that room. I woke up every hour or so, stood up, stared at them, and tried to make sense of what we had done. I thought that it was just the dead of night why my brain couldn't connect any logic to the reality of how 9 months before, Addyson didn't exist and then there she was in our bed- from nothing to life. But I've never been awake enough to wrap my brain around life and living.

Carsyn surprised us 13 months later. Two babies, two baby rooms, pink and purple everywhere. Bows and skirts, stuffed animals and onesies. Tiffanni loved being a mom. She could get both of them laughing long before *What To Expect* said they were supposed to be. Every night I would walk into their rooms and just stare. Life lives here. The experts said that they couldn't keep a blanket on them, so we were to dress them in their blankets. I love onesies. Zipping them up into their "blanket" every night before bed, right after a bath, clean, soft and perfect. We were lucky, our kids just slept. For hours. I would usually visit several times a night just to watch them sleep and breathe and grow. In the moonlit rooms, eyes adjusted to light and life, my babies, our creation- the greatest thing I had ever done.

Brayden surprised us too. Not a surprise in that, I know how it happens, just a surprise in that, oh, this happened. We had just finished building our first house. Moved in in November and Brayden made his grand entrance, or exit depending on your perspective, in January. Bray tried to be stubborn and not sleep for a couple of nights. (Some friends of mine told me about a book called the *No Cry Sleep Solution*, with Amazon reviews attesting to its borderline abusive strategy, I picked it up.) Third babies suffer through a different criteria of parenting. The book said, "Let them cry. They'll learn your schedule." So I did. But that little jerk with foghorn lungs was too loud. Tiffanni begged me to go check on him. "We can't. The book says it's like starting over each time."

"What if he's choking?"

"Then he's probably not crying." I had to come up with someway that she wasn't so alarmed by his crying. So I did what every parent would naturally do, I put his bed in the closet and shut the door. Then shut his bedroom door. Then shut my door. And peace reigned. Not even his fire alarm cry could penetrate all of those doors. And we slept. It took two nights and he was sleeping through the entire night. Hopefully DHR isn't reading or the statute of limitations has passed.

Don't get me wrong, I stood and stared over him and watched him sleep just like the girls. I would bend over the crib rail and hold his hand. And his fingers would instinctively curl around my finger. Warm and soft, oblivious to anything in the world, life in my hand.

I still go to their rooms and hold their hands, watch them sleep. I have to be careful because sometimes it plays to my fears of loss, but there is no greater time of day to stop and be still and breathe in life.

With Tiffanni, some days are hard. Her needs are exhausting and her new quirks often exasperating. She needs help all day long, every taken for granted chore. Each night we start her bedtime routine. A bath, teeth brushed, she insists on chap stick, and medicine. We get her changed and a last chance to use the bathroom, and I walk her to the bedside where she waits on me to brush the unseen, imaginary crumbs off of the bed. I turn off the light, turn on the fan, and turn the TV to the Food Network. And around 8pm I tuck her in for the evening. Within minutes, her body has stopped moving and has settled in for the night. And she sleeps.

I look at her and unlike my kids, where I feel the moment and dream of the future, with Tiff the past comes rushing back and I remember it all at once. With each breath she inhales and exhales romance and giddy and star-crossed lovers, dates and anniversaries and babies, moments and vacations and rendezvous, touches and desire and exhilaration, all that once was and the memory of all the "will be's" that won't. Twenty years worth. In that moment, in that space, the pain escapes and the stillness settles. My daily frustrations forgotten, an anticipation of the next day's concerns yet to begin, and the moment suspends- it's easy to love a baby.

Life is still here. A different kind of life. But life.

TWELVE YEARS AND SOME CARS

The first thing that I ever remember wanting to be when I grew up was a doctor. My uncle asked me when I was about seven years old, "Do you like gummy bears?"

"What are gummy bears?"

"You don't know what gummy bears are? That's a tragedy." And with that we got into his pickup truck and went to the mall. Jelly Belly to be exact. We filled up a trash bag with gummy bears and then he asked me how much I liked jelly beans. "I don't really like them that much."

"Then you haven't had the good ones." Another bag, another cavity, and I headed home with a sugar duffle full of gummy bears and jelly beans. From that moment on, I wanted to be a doctor. Any profession that afforded you the ability to drop everything that you're doing and satisfy your sweet tooth jonesing- I was in.

It didn't last long and I was on to lawyer, professional athlete, police officer, FBI agent, US Marshal (I had just seen *The*

Fugitive), but none of them sat just right. My senior year in high school, the pressure was on and I had to make a decision and nothing made sense.

So many people have voilá moments where the stars align to point to a calling so clear it is unarguable. And maybe it felt that way to many of my closest relationships when it occurred to me that ministry made sense- but the sky never opened up, no dove decensions, no audible voice. It just clicked one day. I think this is what I'm supposed to do. And no one second guessed it. "You'll do great."

At the time I was driving a 1982 Chevy Monte Carlo with a million miles on it. My cousin had given it to me, "No high school senior should be car-less for their senior year!" I loved my first car, some because it wasn't one of my parents' two minivans, and I endearingly named it Hooptie. You had to be the Fonz to make a lot of it work. The radio, the ignition, the trunk, the steering column all had to be MacGuyver'd to get them to cooperate. But the truth was, Hooptie wasn't going to make it to Bible School and I had to work. Which meant that there was no chance of holding a job without a vehicle.

So I did what any kid that had grown up in church would do. I threw out a fleece. "God, you know I need a job. And in order to work a job, I'll need a way to get there. Hooptie won't make it. So, if you want me at Bible School I need some help." And I left it there. I wasn't a fleecer. It always felt like it would backfire, giving God an ultimatum. If I were God, I'd write people off for giving me ultimatums, demanding proof of existence type stuff. At some point, the ever expanding universe, the intricacy of the human brain, the brilliance of life, death, and rebirth through the cycle of seasons, and like, the giraffe are going to have to suffice. But fleece I did.

Just after the baseball state playoffs had ended, I was in my last two weeks of school and came home to an unrecognized car in the driveway. This wasn't odd, with my dad a pastor we regularly had people over. I skipped into the house just in time for dinner and asked my mom who else was joining us. "Joining us for what?"

"Dinner, there's an extra car in the driveway where Hooptie usually parks, and I was curious who was over."

"Your dad and I need to talk to you. Let me get him."

We walked outside and my dad and mom looked at me and said, "A couple in the church heard that you were going to Bible School and said that they believed in you and wanted you to go. Here are the keys." Suddenly I had just upgraded to a 1986 Mazda 323 that would make the trek to Lakeland, FL over the next several years at least a dozen times.

With that, I loaded the car and moved, on my own, 700 miles away to Bible School to learn how to pastor.

This weekend was my 12 year anniversary at Kingwood. 12 years of my over 18 years of youth ministry spent at one church pastoring teenagers. That's a lot of cars and even more teenagers. And somehow, I still love teens. You don't have to be around them long to figure out why. With their faith-testing questions and doubts, their all-in attitudes toward everything from Jesus to Snapchat, their energy and life and love and hope and dreams- I just love being around them. To stare at challenge and loss everyday of my life, I love the medicine of what teens do for my soul.

So, to all of the teenagers that I've been lucky enough to be a part of your life, here at Kingwood for 12 years, and Jackson, Atmore, and Huntsville for over 18, thank you for making me feel like what I do matters. It's one thing for God to give me a 1986 Mazda 323 to confirm that what I will do will mean something, but it's a whole other thing to get you.

TEN MINUTES

Brayden and I walked in the door last night around 5pm after spending the afternoon at Children's Hospital. A little worse for the wear, both of us, he was taken to Birmingham in an ambulance for a neck injury. I came home, tried to eat, and crashed in the bed around 6pm. My adrenaline rush had worn off and my body was exhausted. No damage to the neck, just soreness and a "prescription" for Ibuprofen was amazing news, but my heart and mind were spent.

I got the phone call just after lunch earlier in the day, "Where are you? It's not life threatening, but we're calling an ambulance." I turned on the hazard lights and sped to the school. There's a lot that goes through the mind when you get that phone call. I was stuck 10 minutes away with too little information, too much time, and a current life that doesn't bode well for bad news.

The problem with living this way, it only takes a small trigger to send my mind spiraling. You don't want to know my thoughts during that long 10 minute drive to the school, but I'll tell you this much- if you can imagine it, I thought it.

I got ready to barter with God but remembered that hadn't worked over the last five years. Then I got ready to give God an ultimatum, but was afraid he'd take me up on it.

I've fought for five years to avoid those thoughts. Counseling, exercise, community, prayer, medicine, vacation, sleep, and in an instant, they bored their way into the crossing guard location of my mind policing every other thought. Nothing escapes without being first filtered by fear and loss. You can create an alternate reality in 10 minutes. You can ad hoc a new life. And as bad as those 10 minutes were for me, my kids aren't ready for those moments either. We're just not built for this right now.

As fate would have it, Carsyn walked through the hallway at the same time they were wheeling Brayden into the ambulance. On a stretcher, strapped in from feet to forehead, stabilized, he couldn't move and she broke. Unstable. When you're teetering as is, it doesn't take much to get you off-kilter. I told her all of the things that I wanted to believe like they were facts and then climbed into the ambulance, leaving behind a daughter, face in tear-filled hands, consoled by an eighth grader.

I then called Addyson before she heard it from someone else. Even after starting with, "Everything's ok, I just have to..." she started crying. I grabbed Brayden's hand, juggling emotions, as he looked into my eyes, "I'm scared Daddy." I let Addyson talk to Brayden over the phone so she could make him smile. She's amazing. Then we called Carsyn for another pick me up. They just get it. It's us.

I guess this is as real as I get here. Welcome to the pendulum of my life. The day before, it swings to excitement as I announce my new album and then 24 hours later, backswings to panic. I don't like living with a tilt-a-whirl for an emotional pendulum. Living on the edge gets wobbly sometimes.

The kids stayed up awhile past their bedtime last night. I couldn't send them to bed without stealing those ten minutes back. My heart still heavy, finally lightened by the sound of three voices laughing and loving. I can't control what my mind does every minute of my life, but the moments it wants to go off script, I'll rewrite. I don't know what part of my sanity those few misused minutes cost me in the long run, but last night I exchanged them for a better ten- ten where we held each other tighter, laughed a little louder, and loved a lot harder. For at least ten extra minutes.

ONE QUESTION, TWO QUESTIONS, THREE QUESTIONS, ONE

It took me years, but I know how to get my kids to a place where it's time to talk. They really don't need much. Undivided attention, unconditional love, and some time. For us, bedtime, car rides, dinner alone, a church service with unhurried space at the end, a walk- they all share a few things in common: no rules on subject, no distractions (like cell phone demons), no sense of schedule. Then they talk. Fun talk, serious talk, us talk. It's all sacred.

When I'm functioning at my best, I intention those moments. When I'm a little above average, I at least notice them. But of late those moments are often painful- wrought with doubts and onerous questions. Really the same question, sifted through a filter of age and understanding. Over the last week, just seven days (five to be exact), I've fielded these three questions.

On Saturday Brayden and I were eating guacamole. There's something soothing about palming an avocado pit and letting it slink across my fingers. It has to be a very ripe avocado, not those hard green ones. "Why did we have to get a crazy mom?" he asked between bites. There's a little bit of translation work to be done with an eight year old boy.

"What do you mean, buddy?"

"Out of all of the moms in the world, why does our mom have to be crazy?"

"Do you mean, why does she have a disease that makes her different?"

"Yeah."

"I don't know, pal. I sure do hate it though, don't you?"

"Yeah. I wish she didn't have to be crazy."

A couple of days later, Carsyn came to me with a quivering lip. Even I notice those. Tiffanni used to ask me, "Did you see what that girl was wearing?"

"I didn't even see a girl," I usually responded. The S in my MBTI profile stands for Scant.

Carsyn asked, "Doesn't He know how hard it is for an 11-year old to not have a mom?" You see, these questions have no preface. We start there. I have to switch on my translator and empathizer instantaneously.

"He does baby, He knows it's hard."

"Then why doesn't He do something?"

"I don't know, baby. But I know it's super hard for you." And then she softened the sleeve of my shirt with her tears.

Addyson wasn't far behind with her question that week. There's no off-days here. Instant in season and out.

"Has God ever healed anyone of Huntington's Disease?"

"I don't know, baby. I've never heard of it, but the world is pretty big."

"I sure wish God would heal mom. Why doesn't he?"

"I don't know."

"It's not fair."

"No, it's not fair." And she burrowed her face deep into the space between my collarbone and my cheek. Her safe space that day. The consolation prize to her unanswerable question.

Five days.

Two things that I've learned about the questions lately. First, they're all the same question. The same one question. "Why?" They articulate it in a hundred different ways, but they all fly-by, circle, and finally land on the same runway- why? Second, none of the questions need answers, really. They just need to be asked and then to be heard. Most of the time, anything more than an "I don't know" simply misses the point. The truth is that I would simply ramble until I barely satisfied my own need for an explanation anyway.

So, they ask their questions. Or question really. And I answer. Or don't really. Why? I don't know. But I do know that they need to ask them and I need to hear them. I need to hear in that question that my kids are dealing, dealing the right way. Not that there's a wrong way, but there's a refuge there in those questions- a place where my fear of the kids not making it out of this thing normal is met with the solace in knowing they remain normal when asking this most fundamental, universal question of humanity- Why? And ironically in that simple question, we make it another week. Normal.

PREACHER'S KIDS

"You're going to love it. We'll be 30 minutes from Disney World," they said. The summer between my 7th and 8th grade year, we moved to Central Florida. I left every friend that I had ever known with Mickey Mouse as my consolation prize. My dad, off to Bible College to follow the call with Mom and four kids in tow, we lived in the centipede grass Sahara for a couple of years.

After four schools in four years, I landed just north of Huntsville for 10th grade where I donned my brand new title- preacher's kid. But for some reason, I didn't want anyone to know. I don't think that I was embarrassed of it, I think that I just wanted to start from scratch. If I was starting over, for the third time, I wanted to write the script. No one from our new church went to my school, so I got to learn from past new beginnings and create my own identity. In between frog incisions during biology that first month, a guy asked me what my dad did for a living. "He's in Life Insurance," I said. "We moved to Hazel Green, AL because my dad sells life insurance." Because, well, he kind of was. Life insurance seemed generic enough to avoid a label and give me my best shot, and frankly, was pretty quick on the spot.

When Thanksgiving came a couple of months later, my parents asked me if I wanted to go to Preacher's Kids Camp. My denomination thought that it was helpful for middle and high school kids with similar life experiences and issues to get together and bond over a holiday weekend- long before Black Friday. It was.

I don't know what I expected 25 years ago at the camp, but it felt liberating to not have to hide who I was. Whether or not the label pigeon holed me into someone that I didn't want to be didn't really matter there- we were all in the same hole. I met new friends, new pastors, youth pastors that I was enamored by (one even showed me his for real third nipple, just above his naval), and most importantly a 14 year old blonde who laughed at everything that I said. I followed her around most of the weekend because, well, I don't really know. I don't have the ability to remember those thoughts without filtering it through the last 20 years of my life anymore. Maybe I was just attracted to her easiness of being, or maybe I was attracted to the way that she made me feel about myself, that what I said was really funny, or maybe we were just star-crossed lovers destined to find each other one way or another. What I do remember is coming home and telling my friend Matt that one day I was going to marry her.

I asked Addyson (my 12 year old) a few months ago if she wanted to go to Preacher's Kids Camp. I had just gotten the letter from my denomination, I imagine the same way that my parents did. Her eyes lit up, "Can I? That's where you and mom met." It wasn't a question. It wasn't an anticipation of a love connection- at least not for her. She did, however, seem to want to connect to Tiffanni's and my past. The story of another life, a normal life, long before her memories could delve. And so last weekend she went to camp. Camp for all of us life insurance salesman's kids. Twenty-five years later, she stayed at the same campground, ate in the same cafeteria, and played in the same rec hall that her parents did. She got to listen to another preacher's kid (my brother Joel) share his stories of what it was like growing up as a PK, and be reminded of God's deep and audacious love for her.

I won't pretend to make any predictions on Addyson's life based on what happened last weekend. That campground holds enough significance to me for a lifetime. But what I am fully aware of is that moments matter. Those moments that seem random and coincidental at the time might just hold inside of them life altering implications. What once was seemingly happenstance now feels suspiciously providential. And sometimes moments conspire against luck and campgrounds become the setting for a brand new once upon a time. As my kids struggle through their unspoken doubts that there ever was once a normal life, it's the concrete experiences of our past, the ones that they can see, and touch, and feel, that assure them, maybe this will all work out ok.

A VIEW FROM THE TOP

I still haven't caught up on all of the text messages, Facebook posts and messages, voicemails, and cards. I haven't had time to think about turning 40. I know that it's a big deal for a lot of people, but I just haven't thought about it yet. What I have thought about is how lucky I am.

Last night I got to play the music that, honestly, I stumbled into writing. For years before, I always wanted to record some music. I had written several songs and even tried to record them, but it just never worked out. One night about five years ago, I was in the shower thinking, which is where a lot of my better thoughts are born. At the time, I had a close friend who lived in Nashville who was playing for several different people around town. Somewhere mid-lather, rinse, repeat I thought, "I need to call him and just see if he has any connections. You never know, what if he knows someone." I gave him a call one night and explained my shower thoughts to which he replied, "As a matter of fact, I'm at someone's house right now that I think would be a perfect fit for you. Let me see if he's interested." I drove up two days later and started a relationship with my friend Sean that has now produced over 40 recorded songs.

Music for me has been an outlet and an escape. A place to create and listen, write and reflect. And maybe that's what art is for everyone, for me it has been redemptive. Without the time spent sitting with each emotion, trying to put onto the page what I think that I'm feeling, I'm not sure that I would ever recognize the process. The process of grief, and love, and therapy, and aging, and living, and raising kids.

So, last night I was surrounded by my entire family, by so many in my church family, teenagers and now adults that have been a part of our ministry and lives for years. And each one of them there to exchange their unbelievably above average love for my average songs. And that's really been my life. What I have to offer has always been met with exponentially more in return. Not that I don't love well, I do, but I am loved back in a way that overwhelms me.

If 40 is the top of the hill then I suppose I'm supposed to see the past and the future with the best perspective. But I just don't. The past is clear, filled with love and grace and life and meaning. Not a season without a meaningful moment. The future on the other hand is pretty foggy. It doesn't seem to get clear until it's in my rearview and only when I give myself the time to think about it. Which is what this space has been for me. Each of you, part of my journey of reflection- making sense out of life. I don't know what my next 40 years hold, I don't even know what my next year holds. But I do know that these past 40 years are drowned in goodness. And from up here, the view is brilliant.

TRADITION

There's a commercial on television where a love-struck guy saves all of the chewing gum wrappers from a girl that he likes for years. The day they meet, the day they go on their first date, when they get engaged, married, have a baby, and then they're old and have a bunch of gum wrappers. I'm afraid that I've drained all of the sentimentality out of the scene on accident, it really is cute. But I don't have a sentimental bone in my body. I don't save anything, I have no keepsakes, no affinity toward nostalgia in regards to stuff. I have to remind myself regularly to take pictures because I know that I'll want to remember what my kids looked like when they were younger.

Traditions on the other hand, there's something about an event that we do over and over that melds itself to my sense of importance. I don't know the difference, one is things the other is events, but whatever it is, one I get, the other I don't.

When we were growing up, my parents wouldn't let us open a gift before Christmas day. There those presents sat, under the tree, begging to be opened and played with. My grinch parents held their ground and we waited until Christmas morning. But not Christmas morning officially, technically- we also couldn't come out of our rooms until 6am, so I would just lay there from about 3am staring at the ceiling until 6am rolled around. I think that I pushed them on each of the rules, but of course now do the same thing with my kids. Because it's tradition. We always eat ham for Christmas and turkey for Thanksgiving. It's tradition. We usually went to the same handful of places for family vacation, all ate at the dinner table most nights, got loads of candy one way or another on Halloween. Tradition. Every first day of school my mom wrote me a note in my lunch and on Valentine's Day, mom put some special candy in my lunch. Tradition.

I don't know what it is about traditions that I like, but I just do. They ground me, connect me to something transcendent, bigger than myself. The calendar marks meaningless events until we build a routine around them that makes them matter to us, to our family. I don't remember Christmas generically, I remember hot cocoa, Christmas Eve candlelit services, and Sees Candy. I remember traditions.

So, I have tried to be very purposeful about traditions in my family. On Mother's Day we stay in our PJ's and go get breakfast before church. On birthdays I take the kids out to eat individually. I have a journal for each of them that I write a note in on special occasions. And the first weekend of November, I take Tiffanni, Addyson, and Carsyn to the Christmas Village and then out to eat at the Melting Pot.

This weekend we spent the better part of Friday at Christmas Village. An estrogen extravaganza of crafts, fluffy fashions, personalized knick knacks, and chip dips. Walking every aisle, Tiffanni in a wheelchair for all of our sanity, and the girls darting in and out of every booth that offered a free sample. It was the fifth year in a row and I almost surprised them- only my crew thinks about Christmas the first week of November. Even my birthday has been drowned in eggnog.

After our fill of elf-shaped door hangers and earthen ware ornaments, we left Santa's temporary home and headed to The Melting Pot. Both of my girls will tell you that it's their favorite restaurant. And it's not because of the food. It's because of the tradition.

Tradition centers us. It reminds us of who we are, who we have always been. Some parts of our lives have changed, but we can always come back to these moments. The unchanging moments that keep us together and reinforce stability. Traditions are the events that protect us from the feeling that our world is falling apart because everything seems like it is not as it should be. How we relate, how we eat, what bedtime looks like, who drives who to practice, who fixes meals, what shows we watch together (because the TV is apparently stuck on Food Network), and who prays for the kids at bedtime. The traditions point out to the kids that everything isn't different, there are still these moments when life is simple and good and peaceful. And somehow navigating a wheelchair through a flood of humanity during the first weekend of November, humming carols and begging for sample fudge, quiets the longing for a better day and instead reminds us that the beauty and simplicity of yesterday just isn't that far away.

CONNECTING THE DOTS

I only met Glenda once. "I really want you to meet my mom before we get married." It was a request from my fiancé to be fully known, fully accepted. As Tiffanni and I walked through the doors of the nursing home, the bleached, putrid smell tidal waved my senses. They say that the sense of smell is most closely tied to the memory. We entered her single room, pictures adorning the walls, and I spotted this tiny, broken woman lying on a bed low to the ground. Tiffanni skipped over to her mom, sat down on the bed beside her and began stroking her mother's hand. "Hi momma, I'm here. It's Tiffanni." She talked to her. Sang to her. Asked her questions that she would simply answer herself. It was a one-sided interaction as far as I could tell, but oh the feels.

We left the room, walked through the exit doors, and I broke. Not a quiet, solemn cry. Tears streamed down my face and Tiffanni intuitively grabbed me and consoled me. The wounded healer. "Are you ok?" she asked.

"No. How do you do that?"

"I guess it's all I've ever known." When you watch the slow progression of aging and disease, I suppose it's not such a shock to a system. But to be thrown into the middle of the end was more than I could take. Nursing homes are brutal.

* * *

Tiffanni doesn't do well with details anymore. The truth is that sometimes her memory is sharp and her cognition at least follows a basic train of thought, but she regularly misses the details. She talks to her dad most every day. In fact, I checked her phone and she calls him between 10-20 times a day. She has no idea. I secretly get a kick out of it. Most Thursdays she goes out with her parents. It's clockwork in her mind, but Sunday night she told me that her dad was coming by the next day, Monday. I asked her why he was coming by and she didn't know.

* * *

Ron told me about five years ago that the hardest battle that he remembered fighting with Glenda, was getting her to stop driving. So, when Tiffanni had her final accident, forgetting to put the minivan in park and chasing it into the neighbors garage where it rolled unmanned, I called her dad. "I can't let her drive anymore. It's not safe for her, the kids, or anyone else. Please come help me tell her." Four and a half years ago, Ron and I sat on the back deck of the house that Tiffanni and I built together and took away her independence. It wouldn't be the last thing that I would take, but I remember it the most. We all cried. It was the first thing that her disease would steal. A sign of a selfish interchange that is ongoing in our house- this disease takes only what is good and gives only what is evil. A one-sided devil.

* * *

At 5am on Monday morning Tiffanni woke me. My coherence is limited at that particular 5 o'clock. She was in a panic. "Jerm. Jerm. Wake up." I grunted and pleaded with her to go back to bed. She doesn't compromise well. "Jerm, wake up." Realizing that there was no chance in going back to sleep, I sat up and gave her my best passive aggressive death stare. She is either impervious to those reactions or just stubborn. Regardless of the concoction, she won. "Why is dad coming over today?"

"What are you talking about?"

"Why is dad coming over? He said that he was coming over but didn't tell me why."

"I have no idea. You probably misheard him." And her eyes welled up with tears. Even in my REM-arrested stupor, I spotted them. "What is wrong?"

"Are you putting me into a nursing home?"

I could tell you that that's never crossed my mind, but you know better. But the unlived possibilities of the future, that lurk in the back corners of my mind, discussed only in half-conversations of deep confidence with my closest relationships have never felt real. Surreal sure, but never real. This question stabbed me in the heart. It's one thing to catalogue every possibility in an attempt to find sanity, it's a whole other thing to voice the trajectory of decline. To give it life and breath, a semblance of plausibility.

My mind raced to figure out how we had gotten here. What dots had she connected? What trail of feasibilities had she wandered down, alone, and been left to sink into a darkness of worry? She connected the wrong dots. Sure, dots that all add up to fear, but dots that should have never been placed in a line to begin with.

* * *

One year ago today we began moving into the new house that my parents and I built together. The home that we would redeem my family in. Where we would bring stability, life, love, and hope. Where we would face the faceless future with a certainty of togetherness. This home, our home, that fits us and no one else. Designed with every need we could imagine in mind. A safe place to live our unique lives in wholeness.

* * *

"No Tiff. No one is moving you into a nursing home. We built this house for you. This is your house. We all moved here so that we could live with you. Everyone of us. You're not going anywhere and I'm so sorry that you have worried all day and night about that. You're loved here, and nothing is changing that."

"I was so scared," she told me.

"I bet. Don't keep those worries from me anymore."

And I connected the right dots. Tossed aside the ones that didn't belong in a line, today. The ones that smeared the painting. These dots that we live create a picture that wasn't what any of us planned, but it's a beautiful picture nonetheless.

And sometimes that picture gets blurred and we just have to realign the right dots.

A CRACKER BARRELL EPIPHANY

I had an epiphany. Not quite Moses's burning bush, maybe a little closer to Merton's on the corner of Fourth and Walnut. But that's probably a stretch too.

I grew up in the South. One of the paradoxes of the South is how friendly, brilliantly friendly people can be. I've never stopped and asked for directions that I wasn't given a turn-by-turn Rand-McNally-eat-your-heart-out shortcut. I've even had people get in their cars and tell me, "Just follow me." Only to drive for 15 minutes to get me where I was going. However, we haven't had a great history with race relations, to say the very least.

I didn't realize that I was Southern until I moved to Florida in eighth grade. Kids would come up and just ask me to talk. I couldn't hear the difference in the way that I sounded out words and the way that they did. I'm pretty oblivious to details anyway. Paraded around from group to group, I just liked the attention. Along with my year and a half Florida stint in the nineties, I went to college in Central Florida as well. Not as much parading, but certainly some jabbed parroting.

And somewhere along the way, I heard that Southerners aren't intelligent. I don't know if I ever heard anyone say it directly, but it was implied. From *Saturday Night Live* skits, to the way certain people in the media talked about the South. Monologues and interviews were viewed millions of times on YouTube showcasing our storm-chasers and double-rainbow watchers. Even in seminary, caricatures of old-timey, Holy Ghost preachers were adopted as uneducated. Anyone with an ego like mine, hated that thought. Everyone lives in a bubble of thought and culture, but somehow mine was at the bottom of the totem pole.

Years ago I even bought a book and audio CD of how not to speak with a Southern dialect. If I could eschew my accent, I could unclaim my stereotype. I might have even moved from an 8 to a 7 on the drawl scale. "Enunciate each syllable. Do not hold on to the vowels."

A couple of years ago, I was at Cracker Barrel (obviously abandoning my Southern roots). Along the wall was scattered corn bread mix, chow-chow relish, apple butter, buttermilk pancake mix, jars of fried apples, preserves, jellies, and jams, a peach cobbler kit, peanut brittle, pecan divinity and lemon drops- it was a perfect wall with perfect Southern delicacies and I thought to myself, "I want it all." Like, I really want to buy everything on this wall and go home and eat it. It would seem that while I slept as a kid, my palate was contrived by Cracker Barrel elves. And it occurred to me, "This is who I am. These are my people, this is my home, this is my food."

To be honest, I have never been embarrassed to be Southern. I have been embarrassed to be unintelligent, but I love the South. Like all cultures, we have our dark past that must be laid to rest once-and-for-all, but I love my people. And this week marks the time that I love it the most- the holidays. From Thanksgiving through Christmas, the South is as good as it gets.

Family matters around these parts. And my entire family will be here tomorrow. All of us. In-laws and out-laws, kids and grandkids, even my Australian in-law's parents. This is when we are our best. Around an extended family table that should only sit 12, but we squeeze in more, because everyone wants to be with everyone. We'll eat, and laugh, and tell stories. We'll nap, and shop, and go watch a holiday movie. We'll throw the football, watch some football, and spin kids on the tire swing out back. The food will sit out on the counter all day, because we feel that if we just graze all day, the calories are cut in half.

I had an epiphany at Cracker Barrel a few years ago. Or maybe I just came back around to what I always knew. I'm lucky to be from the South. I'm lucky to be born and raised in a culture that embraces what matters to the human spirit. What makes us who we are, builds our character, and shapes our values. Family.

LIAR, LIAR, PANTS ON FIRE

I was told when I was a kid to not ever ride a motorcycle. So, around nine years old I rode a motorcycle. I was at my friend Chris's house and he had a little Honda 50cc. It beckoned me, begging me to give it a spin. Somewhere between bliss and torture, I had to lay her down.

At nine years old, no one tells you what proper motorcycle riding attire is. I was in shorts, you know mid-eighties Daisy-dukes, and some tennis shoes. That's all. After peeling myself off of the ground the reality of my strawberry covered body hit me. The physical pain was what I was least afraid of.

For the next several days of that hot summer, I trendset early 90's grunge and wore jeans and a flannel. Hiding my full-body scab from my parents was hard and I wasn't able to pull it off for long. My mom gasped when she saw me with my shirt off for the first time and I had to think fast, "I fell down."

"Jeremy, you're scraped up all over your body."

"Yeah, I was running really fast." A top shelf lie.

My dad called me out on my lie pretty quickly and even accused me of riding a motorcycle, "God told me." I could tell early on that Dad, a former man-of-the-world, was gonna be a hard one to pull stuff over on. He punished me by having me memorize Bible verses about how liars were going to spend eternity in hell. I didn't come out of my room for three weeks. Apparently there's a lot of verses about that.

I learned my lesson. There's not much worse in a relationship than lying. It's not the lie that is the problem. That's forgivable. It's the fact that so many statements will be doubted from that moment forward. What's there to build upon? Trust is broken.

I forgot to put money under Brayden's pillow a few years ago after he lost his 3rd or 4th tooth. Look, that's like 30 teeth in all between the three of them and at some point, I just don't care. He came storming into my room after the 3rd frustrating night of placing it under his pillow. "Dad! The tooth fairy gypped me again!" I had relied on his inability to sleep soundly in one position the first two nights and told him that the tooth fairy couldn't find his tooth because he moved so much. But I could sense that he was getting weary of that excuse. So I thought quickly- because that always works.

"No, the tooth fairy came. She left the money in my wallet on the dresser because she couldn't find your tooth again. Get it."

He opened my wallet and said, "There's a ten dollar bill and a one hundred dollar bill."

"Oh, it's definitely the ten." Backfire. Who keeps money in their wallet anymore anyway?

That was an even tighter web of deceit. Lies to cover my lies.

I put Tiffanni to bed last night after a challenging bath time. She just couldn't stay still. "I'm so excited, aren't you?" she asked me.

"What about?"

"I'm getting better." And she stared into my eyes. I can only guess that she was looking for a confirmation. Something to accelerate her belief. Or maybe the question just cold-cocked me in such a disorienting way that I felt it more as a question than a declaration of her own perceived reality.

"You sure are," I stuttered as the words fumbled out of my mouth.

I guess it was Darwin or some shrink that first coined the idea of Fight or Flight. In the survival of the fittest, when your back is against the wall, you fight or you run away. In almost twenty years of ministry, I've seen a lot of people run away. Their desire to be just shuts down. They give in to life's unfortunate lot and accept the hand that's dealt. Which is of course completely understandable. I shut down some days too.

But not Tiffanni. She's a fighter. She wants to go, and do, and be, and breathe. She wants to shop, and eat, and call on the phone, and go on dates. She wants to live. But her body is her archenemy. As stubborn as she is, it fights and she punches it right back. Her sheer determination to live a normal life is equal parts inspirational and discouraging. This would be so much easier if she just gave up. There would be no dissonance between her reality and my reality. What she sees and what I see. But she can't. And I love her for it. Or in spite of it.

So she fights and I lie. "Yes, you're getting better." "No, you're not moving much." "Yes, I understand." "No, everything is great." Because I guess I've come to the conclusion that there's something different about lying to your parents and breaking relationship, and lying to your wife to try and save it.

NOW I LAY ME DOWN TO SLEEP

Adjusting to a new normal has become a regular occurrence around here. Four steps backward, one step forward, and a dozen steps sideways makes for an interesting dance on paper and it makes for chaos in real life. I try not to compare myself to others in similar situations, and yes, there are so many who are, but I stink at this some days. I get it, maybe we'd all stink at this, with a few outliers doing worse, so I can feel a little better. But still, I stink at this some days.

I don't explode as much as I think I'm going to which becomes a win on those days. I haven't grounded one of my kids from life for a month yet, or left my dog in his cage all day, all in a reaction to my anxiety. I can tell when my patience is out of gas and even know how to step away for a few minutes most of the time.

If only medicine worked the same way everyday. Some days I wonder if Tiffanni even needs it and others I want to crush entire bottle up and mainline it into her carotid. Should she it for her or for the rest of us?

The "science" behind getting the right medicine combination feels more like a cross between eenie-meenie-miney-mo and necromancy. Huntington's affects movement, mood, and cognition, but we've yet to get the concoction that addresses all three in a positive way. We get one symptom right and the other two are worse for the wear.

Lately, movement is as good as I can remember it. We've gotten a mixture of pills that has somewhat stilled her erratic movement, so much so, that people have made mention of it. "She's doing so much better!" So I smile and go along with the optimism. I'm not sure what my role is in those moments usually. Yes, her movement is better, but there's a tradeoff. Mood and cognition have taken a hit and I'm stuck with the responsibility of making the decision- what's right for this family? Is it better that she stumble through the house, falling and bruising daily while her mood strikes a balance, or do we still her stagger and allow her to cry all day, connecting events from an alternate reality that her brain lives in?

All of this has proven too much for my brain over the last couple of months. I feel a geyser rumbling on the inside conspiring with my emotions to explode at any moment. What used to settle the inevitable eruption, a jog or a shower, a movie or a book, lacks the alleviation it once had.

So, I've resorted to prayer. Every night after a trying bedtime routine, I feel like I'm a dad of a young child again that has to check for monsters in the closet and under the bed, retrieve a glass of water, read a bedtime story- anything to belabor the impending end of the day. We check each item off of the list and then I sit down beside her, lay my hand on her head, and pray. Nothing elaborate. Nothing revolutionary. In fact, it probably has more to do with the slowing process than the providential one. But in those brief moments, my soul smooths. The tempest's waves of the day fade briefly, and regardless of what Tiffanni has done that day, that hour, the chaos quells, for a moment.

Does prayer change God or does prayer change me? I can't answer for the creator of the universe and honestly feel presumptuous thinking about it. But I am certain of one thing. I know it changes me. At the end of a tough day, a challenging day, to say those few words- slowly, thoughtfully- shifts things. I don't do everything right, but an open invitation into a partnership with God, His bidding, my answering provides a fresh start. Not from scratch, but back a few steps closer to the "I do." Maybe it's just another trial concoction, or maybe it's just a long time coming.

HALF A LIFE WITH THREE GHOSTS AND AN ANGEL

My very first trip to Alabaster after Tiffanni and I started dating was to see her church's production "The Gospel According to Scrooge." A reimagined take on the classic *A Christmas Carol* by Charles Dickens. Tiffanni was very sad that she couldn't be in the musical, "I've been in it every year since I can remember. I played the very first Tiny Tim." But we were off gallivanting at college six hundred miles away, just a bit too much of a commute for her to make practices. It was December of 1996.

We watched and laughed, and true to form, she talked me through the whole thing. "Watch this," "Here comes a funny part", "I love this kid playing Tiny Tim." We hadn't dated long enough yet for her to learn my pet peeve of talking through movies and shows. Not that that would have any bearing on the rest of our lives.

We spent three Christmases together before we were married and each one continued the new tradition of watching Scrooge. In 1999 we moved to Tennessee and Tiffanni presented our pastor with a fun idea- "Let's do a mini-production of Scrooge."

She taught songs and parts and we covered the sanctuary with fake snow and streamers. It's hard to compete with a cast and crew of over 100, but she treated it like we were Broadway and the President was coming to watch.

Each new place, new church, another collaged version of her childhood tradition. Tiffanni adores Christmas. Every year that we have been married, she's asked to set out Christmas decorations earlier and earlier. We once put them out before Halloween. Another time we never took the Christmas tree down because we were in an apartment and I didn't know where to store it- so I didn't fight her. We moved into our brand new home that we built that November the 1st and took the tree straight from one Living Room to the next. She begs for Christmas carols in August, hot chocolate in September, and decorations by October. I think in another life she was the ghost of Christmas present.

When we moved to Alabaster in 2004, the first thing that she said to me was, "Now I get to be in Scrooge!" Nothing made her happier. Addyson was six months old and I kept her while Tiffanni sang her Christmas carol heart out. Each year, as the children came of age (old enough to be in the play, I mean, what else would it mean?) they joined the cast. They set themselves up all year to tryout for a new part. My long-suffering family has driven down and over for years to come be a part of our tradition. We sing and act and dance and laugh. It's a part of our family and my kids don't know Christmas without it.

Last month I turned 40. And it just so happens that I've spent half of my life with Ebenezer Scrooge, "Thank You Very Much", and the Cratchit family- twenty years with that first Tiny Tim. However, I've spent the last five years with three ghosts. A ghost of Christmas Past that reminds me of what was and heckles me at what should be. A ghost of Christmas present that changes daily. The reality of our world constantly adjusting to a new consequence of a tiresome foe. And more and more lately the all too familiar ghost of Christmas Future. The most haunting and unnerving of the disembodied.

This year I felt the ghost of Christmas Future the most. The spirit followed me around the entire production. Tiffanni, unable to be on stage without help, she sang the first song and the last. All dolled up for 10 minutes, she spent the middle of the production in my office watching Christmas movies on Netflix. Each year, a little less, and at some point, not at all. I even caught myself more than once imagining what it would take to build a wooden wheelchair to prolong the inevitable.

Somewhere along the way Scrooge just became a part of our family. The other four of us grafted into Tiffanni's elaborate childhood nostalgia. Reliving old memories and making new ones. I've spent half of my life with three ghosts and an angel. Remembering the past, living the present, and speculating the future. Each ghost leaving their mark on how we view the moment. I'd love to wake up and it all be a dream, able to learn and change and grow from an alternate lived reality, but that's not my story. So, we'll live this one. "God bless us, everyone."

WHY I WRITE

I didn't come to reading easily. There was too much to do, too many words to say. Of course, after going to school for over twenty years, I've finally read a few books, and actually like it. But it didn't come easy. The first book that I ever remember finishing was *A Wrinkle In Time* by Madeleine L'Engle. It was also the first book that I ever read to the kids. Reading takes work. There's a reason that it's easier to sit in front of the television than it is to read. So, for a lifelong shortcutter, reading didn't come easily.

I didn't realize it at the time, but discovered along the way that my favorite genre of books is the Bildungsroman. I won't make you look it up- it's the "coming of age" story. (I love to follow the story of a character grow up.) The journey. *The Outsiders, The Lion, the Witch, and the Wardrobe, The Hobbit, The Catcher in the Rye, The Chosen, To Kill a Mockingbird, Tom Sawyer,* and of course why so many of you love *Harry Potter*. There's something about following the young protagonist through the journey of growth, the tension of development, that gets me every time. At the end of the day, there's only about seven stories to tell, and "Coming of Age" is my jam. Tell it a million different ways and I'll read it a million different times.

I'm not 100% sure, but my guess is that the more someone reads, the more likely they are to begin to ask the question, "Can I do this?" I know that I have. Can I write? It's a highly presumptuous question. I have several different friends who are accomplished writers. I have one friend who has a book with a foreword by Alice Munro who calls her a "brilliant writer." Alice Munro! As in the Nobel Prize Alice. Everyone can't write, so I don't want to ever presume upon my friends that are professional writers that I can do what they do, what they've spent a lifetime of crafting and honing to do. That would be like someone coming up to a NASA scientist and saying, "I've shot fireworks before, scoot over and let me show you how to build a space shuttle."

A few years ago, I wanted to see if there was anything to this desire to write. So, I went back to school at our local liberal arts college to take some classes on writing. I met a couple of amazingly gracious professors who helped me to explore. I asked questions, fumbled through stories and poetry, read about writing, talked about writing, learned about writing, and wrote. I started rough and finished a little better.

Last year, I realized that this journey with Tiffanni was flying by. I got caught up in the everyday minutia of life. Relationships strained, tedium mounted, normality waned, and days checked off the calendar as if they had never been lived. "One day at a time" became a mantra that was less about living each day and more about tolerating it. This isn't an okay way to live. So I began to write.

I wrote to notice. I wrote to notice the life that was lived in between meals and baths, morning times and bedtimes, ballgames and school presentations, church services and workdays, school dropoffs and pickups. But more importantly, I wrote to notice the life that was lived inside of those moments. A lot of life gets lived in the mundane. The average, everyday moments- the non-Facebook worthy moments. And hundreds of them were passing me by without so much as an acknowledgement.

So, I write. It is a sacred act of spiritual discipline for me. Without it I miss God in the silence. I miss the joy of my children in the monotonous. I miss the love of my wife in the routine. I miss the gift of every relationship in the casual. I miss the fulfillment of my work in the required. I miss the spirituality in rest. I miss the holiness in sharing a meal with a close friend. I miss the peacefulness of my often chaotic home. I miss the sacrifice of my parents. I miss the joy of a simple telephone call from my brothers and sister. I miss the medicine of laughter. I miss the gratification of finishing a home. I miss the contentment of my life. I can't afford to miss those things, for they are life. So, I write to notice life. A beautiful life. And this is my Bildungsroman.

LIVING A DREAM

I mostly blame it on her college roommates. A conspiracy to steal my greatest commodity. A simple warning would have been nice. Tiffanni and I had only been married a week the first time it happened. I was jarred from a deep REM cycle by a piercing whisper. The kind that cuts through silence and has more in common with a scream than a hush. We were in our brand new apartment, middle of the night, sound asleep. Or so I thought. "Someone is in our room," She breathed into my ear. "Someone is here." That statement could kill a coma.

"What?! Where?!" A panic surged up my spine. I hate being scared. I was never a horror movie guy. Some of my friends loved to be frightened out of their minds- *Halloween*, Jason, Freddy, Steven King books at night- that was never me. I got talked into watching *The Exorcist* when I was in High School with a bunch of friends. I don't speak to any of them anymore.

"Right there, in the shower, just behind the curtain. Go get him." Unfortunately, the age of feminism hadn't reached the dirty South yet, so it was my duty to do something. "Do something, you're the man," she reminded me. I tiptoed to the bathroom and threw back the shower curtain. Nothing. I turned to see what Tiffanni was doing and she was passed out. Jerk. We talked about it the next day and she didn't remember a thing. One of the scariest moments of my life, she just concocted and then slept right through. "Yeah, Candy (her roommate) told me that I talked in my sleep a lot. Like every night."

"And no one thought that was pertinent to our 'for better or for worse'?" Over the years I figured out how to play with her in her sleep. I figured that I owed her. Once I even followed her to the kitchen pantry. She was digging in the bottom of the closet where we kept a bag of potatoes. "Whatcha doing?"

"I'm looking for my pants."

"Did you hide them in the potatoes?" And with that she stuck her tongue out at me and went and got back into the bed. We've had entire conversations in her sleep. And she remembers nothing. Regrettably, all of this before the age of one-button-video cell phones.

But a few nights ago, she woke me again. This time it was different. "There's someone in the corner. I felt his hand on my leg. Do something." I tried to reason with her. Begged her to go back to sleep. But she was adamant. So, once again I got back up and turned on the lights, looked under the bed, searched the closet, the corners, the entire room and bathroom. And nothing. She didn't go back to sleep. For the rest of the night, she woke me every few minutes to check again.

"I have. There is no one here. No one is going to be here." She just couldn't rationalize. The dream was too real and sadly, this disease has affected the all too important area of logic. The next morning, with the lucidity of the daylight I told her about what happened. "You talked in your sleep all through the night. It was miserable. You were scared and confused. You kept thinking that you saw someone in our room."

"I know, there was someone there. I saw him."

This disease doesn't just stay in the realm of the real. It inserts itself into the reprieve of the dreams. An uninvited spoiler to the only respite either of us have some days. There was a time that we laughed about her midnight sleep-walking and sleep-talking, the moments of suspended logic when she collaged the day's random events into an incoherent delusion. Now there is no boundary between the two. If Huntington's affects cognition, it eliminates the buffer that separates the two worlds of reason and imagination. The beauty of dreams become another event that is absorbed into the memory, which is fine when they are beautiful. It's miserable when they aren't as pleasant.

It's hard to imagine what it's like to live in two worlds simultaneously. Unable to separate the land of the real and the land of the distorted. The place where all that you love and all that you fear coexist. The place where your memories are born and the place that those same memories are corrupted. It's hard to imagine living there.
Well, maybe not.

MUSIC OF THE HEART

My kids love Top 40 radio. I guess all kids do. I remember listening to "Yes It's True" by Huey Lewis in the back seat of the squished Datsun carpool ride on the way to 4th grade like it was yesterday. *Back To The Future* melodies and 80's breakdance pop escorted us to the front door of the school where the Safety Patrol convoyed us through the orange cones. 80's simple rock and pop would be the soundtrack of the memories of my childhood until Nirvana could take over in the angst of my high school years. Nostalgia is always rose-colored.

Over the last several years, the kids and I have had some very important conversations about music. "There is music that we like, and then there is music that moves us. And rarely is the music that moves us found on the radio." It's hard for an entertainer to convey the heart behind a lyric that she didn't write. Singers are a dime a dozen, ask any weekend karaoke bar, but lyricists that can capture the intricate tone and hue of human emotion, who incite the imagination, are a rare breed. Sometimes I try to write a song with the sole goal of discovering just one perfect lyric, one heartstruck phrase. Just a few words that resonate with passion and paradox. And then there are the exceptional writers who fill and feel every note with them- every line a burrowed shaft into the soul of human frailty. That is the music that moves us.

A year after Tiffanni was diagnosed, I sat down at a piano to attempt to pen some words of how I felt. That first year was devastating. The disease spread at a brisk rate and it affected every aspect of our life. Her body began to convulse constantly, I had to take her car keys, she couldn't sing anymore with any clarity, dinner party invitations waned, she couldn't cut hair, she couldn't cook- it was overwhelming. So, I sat at the piano and wrote every line of the song in one sitting through tears just to find the line, "I still feel the same." After a few weeks of recording and production, we sat in the car together one day and I told her, "I want you to hear something," and played her "Clearwater Sand" for the first time.

As the song played she sat expressionless. Distracted and clearly unable to focus, she asked me when it ended, "That's pretty, what was it about?" I explained the song and the thought behind it and she responded impassively, "Aw, that's sweet." A disease that steals the emotions might be the most damned presence to ever inhabit the human experience.

Most days I don't want to feel. Or maybe my body knows that I can't handle feelings that particular day. But there are some moments where I need to sense. Where the music that moves me is given freedom to express for me. I have my go-to's. The guys and gals that live out their light and darkness in song and then loan the world the emotions for the rest of us to feel. Those that uncover the melancholy of the world if only to give it a name.

A few days ago Tiffanni and I were driving down the road

and I was listening to one of my go-to's. One of the guys that brings out the feels. Sometimes you just need to feel to validate that you're still alive. Still a part of this thing. Tiff and I usually drive in silence. Sometimes I think aloud so as to imitate a conversation, but for the most part we ride in quiet. Our most common setting. As I glanced over at Tiffanni, tears were streaming down her face. I panicked, what could be wrong. Did she get hurt? Did she forget something trivial? Did she lose something? "What's wrong Tiff? What happened?"

And through her genuine sadness she said, "This song, I don't know why, but it just made me cry."

There are these quaint moments, suspended for a brief second, that I'm able to say, "Oh, there you are. I knew you were still in there somewhere." They are rare. They are found in a smile, a laugh, a wink, a smirk, a tear. The music of the heart. Not just the moments that I like, but the moments that move me. The brief and simple moments that I can honestly say, "I still feel the same."

BORN A MINUTE TOO EARLY

For some unknown reason, I'm fascinated by technology lately. Not current technology, but upcoming technology. I read that by the year 2030 (which sounds so far away, but do the math) there will be so much pressure on people in America not to drive, that we will mostly be a country of self-driving cars. From 30,000 car fatalities a year, to a fraction of that number nearly overnight.

The internet has basically had about three iterations. It started with what is now called Web 1.0. The internet for us was essentially an online encyclopedia. If you wanted to look something up or find something out about a company, like its number and open hours, you could search for it. Then came Web 2.0 which was the social media craze- where you and I began to interact with one another, a borderless world of instant pen-pals. Web 3.0 is called the Internet of Things. Where everything in the world will be interconnected and talking to each other. We're starting to see it in our cars, our thermostats, our refrigerators, our cell phones- I even have a garage door that I can open with my cell phone from anywhere in the world. I'm not sure the usefulness of that, but can any of you open your garage door remotely from Liberia?

In thirteen years, we could have a country filled with driverless cars that communicate with each other to minimize traffic, accidents, and bird flipping. We'll have to figure out another place to channel our road rage. An entire industry will be built on in-car entertainment.

And medical technology will see advancements at a rate that healthcare has never seen. Mark Zuckerberg, you know, the Facebook guy, and his wife just declared their intention to put in place a plan and initiative to cure, prevent, or manage all human disease before the end of the century. Did you see that little three letter word? ALL.

Tiffanni's longtime neurologist just retired a few weeks ago which sent us into a kerfuffle trying to decide where do we go from here. My parents went to an informational meeting with a young Huntington's specialist who asked to see Tiff. So, Friday we have her first appointment with the new guy. But I've heard some pretty amazing things about him so far. I have a former student in medical school at UAB that had a neurology lab with him that she said "inspired her." In that lab he told the students that he believed Huntington's would be the next neurological disease to be cured. In fact, there is a drug that is in Phase 2 testing now that inhibits the disease from ever actualizing. I have no idea what Phase 2 testing is. Could be the rats, I guess. But exciting nonetheless.

It doesn't take a lot to put two and two together about my greatest fear. I'm certain that many of you have thought it and just not asked. Huntington's is a neurological degenerative disease that is passed down through heredity. My children have a 50% chance of having it. I have three kids. The math stinks. The disease typically shows up in the mid-thirties, so I'm in an 18 year window of hope and fear- not sure what the word is for that unique emotion. Eighteen years sounded like a million when I was a kid. Now that I've lived over two of those windows, Time feels like a spoiled brat demanding his way at the Walmart checkout line.

Over the last week my brain has made me think a lot about the finality of this disease. That my kids will hopefully see the end of it forever and that Tiffanni will just see the end. That my kids will see the end of it from one angle and Tiffanni will see the end of it from the other. Like standing on two sides of a chasm. It makes me think of Jack and Rose in the ice cold waters of the Atlantic just after the Titanic sank. I remember thinking as he drifted to the bottom of the ocean, you couldn't wait one more minute? The rescuers are right there!

I once read that thousands of soldiers died after World War II had already ended. They just didn't get the news in time. And I feel this hole in my heart for Tiff. In the grand scheme of the history of the world, she was born just a minute too early. Just seconds before someone arrived with the antidote. Just moments before rescuers rowed up with life jackets and warm blankets. An instant before the pardon came through. This tiny little minute between life and death. All of our lives would have been different. If she, if we, could have been born just a minute later.

THE ETERNAL EMOTION

It never took much to make her laugh.

She said that her dad made her laugh all of the time and that she admired that in a man. A boyfriend. A husband.

"I want to marry someone that makes me laugh. Someone that I can laugh with." That's a lot of pressure. To perform. But it was never hard. It's easy to make someone laugh that wants to. That doesn't have any inhibitions to laughing. Someone whose soul is light.

That's something that I never understood, still don't. How do you go through life watching your mom waste away, become less aware, less present, less engaged, less interactive, and respond with levity. She always had an easiness about her. Easy to love. Easy to fall in love with.

Baggage scared me when it came time to date for real. There were girls with all of the typical stuff, the heavy stuff and it just scared me. But with Tiff there was never anything there to worry about. The inevitable baggage just never showed up. I waited for the shoe to fall and she always kept it on, balancing on two classy heels, dolled up, dressed to the nines. Baggageless.

We laughed a lot.

I can't remember a day going by, for years, that we didn't laugh. There was the time that we discovered her sleep walking. And the time that I walked in on her dressing up our dog in full outfits, setting a scene, and taking pictures- he was a chef, a baseball player, a clown- poor guy. The time that she got peed on in the face by one of our kids- I'll let you guess which one. Or was that twice?

Once we were on a group date with 10 or 15 friends at Disney Village when I jumped into one of the theme pools fully clothed. She was so angry, "When are you going to grow up?" I looked at her like she was an alien.

"Are you serious right now? This is who I've always been. This what you get, take it or leave it." And she started laughing. Not so much at the pool violation, at the person that she had just confused herself to be.

"I have no idea what I was thinking." And she jumped in with me.

We laughed at the songs that she used to sing to me in her funny voice in the middle of the night. I would wake her from a dead sleep and say, "Sing" and she wouldn't skip a beat- she'd start singing from the middle of a REM cycle. Who does that?

We laughed at all of the silly things that our kids said. We laughed at movies and plays. We laughed at weddings and at funerals. We laughed at life and life laughed back.

Our life was light. It was fun, it was funny. We've made a beautiful life together of easy.

Over the last few years, easy has been a little harder to find. Some days are so long and trying. But I've discovered something recently that I hadn't seen in a while. Tiffanni has started laughing again. A lot. It takes a little work some days, but it's there. It just takes a little effort. Every night after we go through our ever-lengthening bedtime routine, I sit down on the side of the bed and stare at her. And then ever-so-slightly, I furrow my brow, just enough that she notices. She tries to hold her smile like a game of Staredown, but I can always detect the nose flare. That's her tell. I know what's coming next. Some nights I can't wait, so I just start tickling. Which is odd because she used to tell me how terrible I was at tickling. Now I can get her every time. She probably just has so many laughs backed up from the last several years, they're bursting to come out.

I don't know all of the emotions that will last for eternity, but I do know one. Buried so deep inside of her, guarded by all that is good, this damned disease can't get to it. She laughs and defies. A rebellion against all of hell. Some days just a smirk, others a tickle, and some a full on belly cackle. All of these other emotions that have wedged their way into our daily lives- fear and sadness, grief and anger, frustration and fatigue, sorrow and discouragement- they have a shelf life. Their time is limited. But laughter. It knows no end. It burrows its way from the ephemeral into eternity where it finds its permanent home. For now, it is the sole taste of the afterlife, the eternal life, that has made its way into our life. And this glimpse of eternity is easy. It's light. And it's good.

ACHING ARMS

I can name about three memories before 2nd grade. My brother Adam being born. Getting chased on the playground by some girls in kindergarten. And Santa Clause-gate, when innocence was stolen, dreams were shattered, and I realized that the exorbitant gift-giving Santa was now on a budget. I just don't know what my kids remember. It all happened so fast. Normal and then nothing close to it. Of course they didn't know things were different- life just was.

Tiffanni and I had only been dating a few months when she found out that her sister was pregnant. She got in the car and drove 400 miles to celebrate. When my nephew was born, she was there. Skipped school for a week. I get that babies are a big deal, she shopped for months leading up to the life entrance. But it surprised me that someone would shop that much for their own kid, let alone another's.

With a backseat filled with toys, clothes, diapers, she debated getting her own carseat, and headed north for the baby event of the century.

It was another few months before I would ever see what the fuss was all about. Babies are cute and all, but they all look and act the same. I'm not sure they even have a personality until about age two- unless you count colic. And then they're just jerks. We showed up and Tiff darted out of the car toward the house and by the time I drug all of the suitcases into the living room, she had my nephew cackling and making new noises that "we've never heard him make before."

Tiffanni was magical with kids. She can still get a kid staring and smiling in Dairy Queen every time. I try to mimic her but I apparently tortured and burned stuffed animals at the stake in another life. Kids can sense innocence. This evolved intuition that discerns the difference between safety and danger manifests in a simple smile or a faint ignore. Tiff could make every kid laugh. Put them all at ease. She was made for children. Patient and kind. Which is why she worked with special needs kids for the first couple of years of our marriage while she attempted to finish school.

Tiffanni was diagnosed with Huntington's in the fall of 2011. My intention was to live as full of lives for as long as we could, until circumstances inhibited us. I planned several trips, several getaways, and unplugged from as much noise as I could. Within three months her dad and I had to ask her to stop driving. It wasn't really a request, not after she drove through the neighbors' garage door with our kids in the backseat. We cried as we realized that this disease was demanding and unforgiving.

The following summer, I was out of town for the day when I got a phone call from one of Tiff's friends. "I don't want to be a tattle-tale, but I just talked to Tiffanni and she told me that she feels better. She feels in control and is tired of sitting around the house. When we hung up she was getting the kids in the car to go to Sonic for happy hour." I panicked. The last time she was driving could have been disastrous and now this. I quickly called her phone from two hours away and did my best calm voice when she answered.

"Whatcha doing?"

"Nothing, why?" I heard the distinct ring of the car key in the ignition behind her voice. The kids laughing.

"Why does it sound like you're in the car?"

"I'm not."

"Tiffanni, I need you to listen to me. Please don't drive with our kids. Please don't drive. I know it's not fair, but you can't drive."

"I wasn't."

"Ok, I'll be home this evening." I hung up and called her dad who was able to go over and help me settle the situation.

The last time she ever got into a driver's seat was to take them to Sonic. And she didn't even get out of the garage.

We've talked, the kids and I, a lot about what they remember. Brayden can't remember a day that his mom was "normal." He asked me one day, "Why did God make mom crazy?" Addyson and Carsyn can't ever remember anything either. I'm sure it's because at some point, the memory begins to jade their recall, stamping all memories with the filter of disease.

So I prompt them. I try to trigger thoughts. We talk about Christmas, which Tiffanni loved- putting the tree up in September. I remind them how she chased them around the house nearly every day. How she tickled them till they couldn't breathe. How she carried them around on her hip so much that people commented on Tiff's biceps regularly. How she dressed them up, made them costumes, did their hair, snuck their makeup. We've lost a lot.

I picked the kids up from school yesterday, a rare day that everyone came home at the same time. Of course they asked to go to Sonic for happy hour. We ordered slushies and limeaids and laughed and told stories. Addyson kept asking me to turn the music up and then reminded herself, "Oh, you want to talk." My almost teenager.

In the middle of our break from life Carsyn got excited and said, "I remember mom checking me out of school. She came and got me and said, 'My arms were just aching for you. I couldn't bear to be without you anymore.' And she took me to Sonic and then to play. Just us."

Addyson screamed, "Me too! She said the same thing, her arms were just aching too much to let me stay in school."

"You guys remember that?" And they nodded. "You were only four and five years old."

"She did it a lot," they told me. And I remembered. She kept one of the kids home from school every off day that she had. She couldn't just take a break, or I suppose the kids were her break. My little truants.

My last memory of Sonic, filled with pain and fear, but

Carsyn's and Addyson's filled with all that was good about their mom. Her aching arms, her contagious laugh, her simple love.

SHE SPEAKS

She tries to furrow her brow, eyes squint, lips pursed. "Like this," I say. I pull my right eyebrow down as I lift my left eyebrow up. I flare my nostrils and compress my lips. She smiles her new smile. An echo of what it once was, but clearly her smile. She tries again, but just squeezes both eyes tightly. Squinched face, wrinkled forehead and I burst out laughing. She smirks. She knows that she's made me laugh and enjoys her accomplishment.

I'm not a morning person. Never was. Neither are any of my siblings. My mom drove us to school every day of my life that I can remember and didn't bat an eye when I asked her to drop me off half a mile from the front of my high school entrance the first day of 10th grade. Mornings were a somber stint. Each kid staring into his bowl of cereal with small breaks to read the back of the box of Cinnamon Toast Crunch only to return to the milk slogged cereal bowl. Zombified, we didn't really wake up until 9 or 10am, long past that expressionless drive to the awkward momzone drop off before lumbering in to first period.

So it was a culture shock those first few years waking up

to chipperfest every morning after we got married trying to pretend that I enjoyed discussing the outfit that I would wear for the day the minute I opened my eyes. "Hey there sleepy head," she would rouse me to cognition before my left eye could even join my right eye, "I've been waiting on you to wake up for so long." And it would begin. A peppering of words and thoughts and ideas and reflections and ponderings before I had time to blink for the first time. My ears and eyes accosted by my sprightly life partner as I struggled to remind myself of my vows.

At some point I remember telling her, "You're going to have to give me a few minutes before you attack me with the morning." Which didn't seem to compute well, except to offer an intermission of explanation to herself in between thoughts.

"Good morning sunshine, guess what crazy dream I had," she would begin. If my eyes worked yet, I would roll them, if not I always had a reclose. "Oh that's right, you're not a morning person, I'm sorry. I'll give you a minute. But before I do, I have to tell you about this crazy dream I had." And the ever-elusive minute never quite actualized. I guess my face sometimes looked like I was awake before I really was because regularly I would open my eyes to mid-conversation and scramble to catch up, dazed and disoriented, reaching for context clues and keywords.

Eventually we reached a compromise. Ear plugs.

I hate grammar police in everyday speech. If you want to correct my syntax after I deliver the State of the Union, fine, but when I'm just telling a fun story and everyone is laughing and enjoying themselves and you point out that I ended a question with a preposition, leave me alone. Sometimes I use the wrong word and someone corrects me. And I just want to scream, "Did you understand what I said? Do you know what I meant? Then I communicated. What I wanted to say, you heard."

Communication is a funny thing. While words matter, correct words, they aren't deal breakers. There are so many other ways to communicate. The eyes convey a language all their own. The body speaks messages that words sometimes can't. Pauses, tone, inflection, speed, volume can all dramatically change the smallest of words and phrases. The truth is that you and I could have spoken a fraction of the words that left our lips today and have gotten across what needed to be said without any misunderstandings.

Words are hard to come by these days. Tiff makes dozens of phone calls everyday and I get dozens of apologies, "I'm so sorry, I just can't understand what she's saying. I keep having to ask her to say it again." She repeats those few worded phone calls over and over just to make the connection. In public, I stand at her side as a translator like we're on the mission field. But the truth is, it's getting harder for me too. I have to use context clues again. If she's holding her brush, I assume that she needs her hair brushed. If she hands me her cup, I'm fairly certain that she's asking me to refill it. She regularly reaches for the volume while in the car and I know that she wants me to talk to her.

After over twenty years there's not a lot that needs to be said with words anymore anyway. A smile, a laugh, a tear, a frown. Empathy is in the eyes. Compassion in the hands. And love in that crazy little eyebrow furrow that she just can't quite get, but she keeps doing it over and over and over because I keep laughing. A million words, a million feelings, a million joys- not one word.

HOME

7th grade was the greatest year of my life. At least up until that point. For an extrovert, my class size just increased exponentially. I went from the same group of friends in every class to having a different group of friends in each class. Each subject was a new adventure in class pranks. There was my geography teacher's velcroed toupee that never matched his eyebrows in color or movement. We tried to land erasers in it without him noticing. My biology teacher's aquarium that we built pencil ships to sail in. Lunch and PE, an excursion from pseudo-learning into pseudo-exercising. English- girl taunting, math- paper wad basketball, and walking the halls- chariot races. I think that I learned something. It was the introduction into a social butterfly's dream. I knew that the next five years would be unbelievable.

The summer before I would begin 8th grade we moved to Florida.

600 miles away from every friend I had ever had.

I started from scratch. Well, not completely from scratch.

I had my trusty Eskimo Spitz named Cotton, two brothers that I still outweighed by 30 pounds and could beat up, and a sister who was four. In no particular order. Except for Cotton. That first year was hard. Making new friends with people that hadn't necessarily reserved space in their worlds for me proved challenging. The first week at lunch I sat with cheerleaders. As amazing as that sounds, it was because I was sitting by myself and they came over because they felt sorry for me. Which is still sweet. I muddled through the year the exact opposite way that I anticipated 8th grade would have gone.

When the school year ended my parents let us go back home and spend the summer with my grandparents. It was an interesting summer. To my surprise, all of my friends had gone on without me. The chasm that I left in their lives with my departure was quickly filled with, well, chasm-filling-stuff. My anticipation of how we would pick up where we all left off was met with a realization that they didn't even realize that I was gone. It's an odd place to live- homeless.

At the end of the summer my grandparents drove us back. We were met by fun-deprived parents and my dad said, "That'll never happen again." I looked at him confused. "This house was too quiet. Every single day we missed you and I regretted letting all of you go. You can't go from a house of six to a house of two overnight. Never again. We just missed you." I didn't get it. I think I still had whiplash from my introduction to the gypsy life.

Tiffanni and I started dating in the same city where several years before I was introduced to loneliness. We lived on a small college campus and recognized nearly everyone. Even before we started dating, our time together increased. I would walk her to breakfast in the morning, find her between classes, meet her for lunch and dinner, and spend every night until curfew doing any number of things. Appropriate things. We were rarely apart. If that wasn't enough, we would usually talk on the phone after curfew for awhile each night until I finally begged off to write a paper or two before we hit repeat the next day. In a city 600 miles away from the only place that I ever knew as home, a city that I never expected to meet a single friend, I found my best friend.

We've spent the last 20 years mostly inseparable. From that first walk across campus to now chauffeuring her everywhere that she goes, we're together a lot. We built a family together which is pretty amazing when you take some time to think about it. There are three kids that exist because she and I fell in love. And because of that, I've fallen in love with my kids.

I don't like it when the kids are gone. Not one of them. The house feels wrong. The dynamic is off because something, someone is missing. I really do want to let them grow up and discover themselves and spend the night out with friends that they could have forever, but I hate it. While they're out making memories, I'm trying to hold on to them. My kids have lived in five different homes with me and Tiff- all in the same city. And I was content in every one. Because they were there. Home was never about a place, a house. It was always about a relationship. We could move a dozen more times and nothing would change. Home is where you're loved unconditionally, where every moment matters, where you pile into the bed wadded up like puppies and watch another episode of *Full House*, where you play bad board games with made up rules, where you break bedtime to tell another story, where you wrestle and laugh and hug and cry. Home is where my kids are. My kids are home. And I'm never letting them go off for the summer.

THE ADVENTURE OF PARADOX

I remember a few things from seventh grade. It was there that Mrs. Norton, my English teacher, made me fall in love with literature and the power of language. Almost thirty years later, I still hear her words:

"A lot" is two words, not one.
People are hanged, pictures are hung.
Judgment does not have an "e" in the middle.
It's theater not thee-ate-er.
Salmon is pronounced sammon, not sal-mon.
Whom is the object of the preposition
And finally, I remember most vividly, she introduced me to Greek Mythology

In *The Odyssey*, the hero Odysseus spends some time as a captive on an island with cyclopes (Yes, I had to look up the plural for cyclops.) When Odysseus and his men arrive at the island of the giants they are befriended by one named Polyphemus, who eventually turns on them, traps them in his cave, and then begins to eat them one by one at mealtime. During one of the evenings, Odysseus and he are talking and

Polyphemus asks him his name. Odysseus replies, "Nobody, Nobody is my name." On the following night, Odysseus drives a stake into the eye of Polyphemus and eventually escapes with his remaining men strapped to the bottom of sheep. As the monster screams for help his friends come and ask him who has done this to him. "Nobody is killing me," he screams. So they return home confused and disinterested. Odysseus is able to escape and eventually make it back to his bride Penelope.

A paradox is something that seems to be contradictory in nature, but is in fact true.

Not to be confused with the comedienne Pete Holmes's "Incredulous Statements" in which he states a basic word several times, peaks your attention to its misplacement, and then reveals his problem with that word.

For instance, Unicorn.

Unicorn?

Really, uni...corn? The animal has one horn. Was it really that difficult to say unihorn?

I live a paradox at times. A life of contradiction, but is in fact true. My life is beyond blessed. I have three beautiful and healthy children. I get to do what I believe I am designed to do and actually get paid for it. Enough money to put me in the top 1% of wage earners in the world. I have always and still have a family that supports me in every way.

But.

But there is a dissonance on the inside of me. Things aren't all as they should be. To live in a paradox is an odd place to live. Where things are as good and as bad as they can be, at the same time. Dickens said, "It was the best of times and it was the worst of times." I live there. I'm watching my children grow from amazing kids into amazing young people. I'm watching my wife just grow older. It's weird to feel blessed and cursed at the same time. To feel joy and pain. To teeter like an egg on the ridge of happiness and sadness. To watch my kids begin to experiment with their personalities as they shape their dreams and futures and then to feel trapped from mine. To feel in the will of God and forsaken by Him at the same time. If things were all black I could bounce and smile and live and thrive. And if things were all white I could curse and cry and mope and die. But things aren't black or white, my life is grey. These life contradictions and paradoxes are grey. Life is a paradox and it's an odd place to live. Not quite the adventure that I anticipated, but an adventure nonetheless in which Nobody is taking care of us.

GAME NIGHT

My brothers and sister and I made up a lot of games when we were kids. We were the last generation without video games, purists of the gaming community. We used sticks, tape, rocks, bricks, and nature. You know, Minecraft outside. Did I say kids? We still do.

As a youth minister, I get to still make up games and try them out on kids. At one lock-in, Joel and I made up Duct Tape Spit Wad, one of our most clever creations. The group was divided into teams, each with five rolls of duct tape, a box of tissue paper, a bowl of water, and about 20 teens. The goal was to tape a teen to the wall and then dip the tissue paper into water and throw the wet wads at the taped teen. The teen with the most spit wads won. You're welcome, parents.

I make up games with my children often. Half of the time it is a ploy to get them to do chores faster. The other half of it is simply entertaining. Myself. And over the past two years we've become board gamers. Like, geek gaming tabletop addicts.

Over the last two years, I've spent some time studying a

personality typing tool called the Enneagram. There are nine types, with deep nuance to each, that each person on the planet most closely identifies with. The brilliance of this tool is that it helps a person discover her mask, coping mechanism, or what Thomas Merton calls, "The false self." The false self is the person that each of us spends the majority of our energy trying to be. It is the person that I think everyone wants me to be, or the person that I believe will benefit me the most, but not my true self. The true self is who I really am. The me that is not motivated by manipulation, but instead motivated by love. The true self is content to be himself. He is not afraid of his limitations and humbly recognizes his gifts as truly gifts. Alice Fryling says, "One of the values of the Enneagram is that it not only identifies the compulsions of the false self, it also suggests the grace that invites us to return to the true self."

At birth, each person is given a gift. It is her gift to the world, the gift by which she makes the world a better place, the place that God intended it to be. But the false self gets scared that this gift is not enough. "People need me to be more. This can't be all that I have to offer." And the gift is replaced by a compulsion, a false gift to supplement the seemingly insufficient true gift. The Enneagram helps us to see this gift, its tendentious compulsion, and God's invitation to return to the true self.

So as not to get too technical, I'll show my cards. Not something that I like to do unless I'm highlighting my brilliance (welcome to the Type 7). I am a Type 7- The Epicurean. The gift that God gave me for the world is joy. To be able to bring contentment, laughter, fun, and life to those around me. Sounds awesome, right! However, often I don't think that what I am contributing is enough, so my compulsion is gluttony. Not gluttony in the traditional sense, but gluttony in the sense of an unquenchable appetite. Life is not joyful enough, so I must breathe in, take in as much life as I can. And I do this through limitless projects, events, outings, creative outlets, relationships, hobbies, ministries, you name it.

Many of you know me enough to know that I can tend to live a gluttonous lifestyle. In case you don't, I'll remind you. Last year I started a blog, recorded an album in Nashville, ran my first triathlon, began writing a book, started a new continuing education class, began a dozen books that I didn't finish, watched every Oscar nominated movie in seven different categories, and traveled out of state about ten times, just to name a few. I have a fear that I won't be able to get all that there is out of life. Major FOMO- "Fear of Missing Out." I have a fear that I will miss out on something, but I also have a strong aversion to anything painful. Any suffering. I must be careful that out of all the things that I try to fill my life with, I am not avoiding the invitation from God into my pain. That He is even there, in the shadow of death. And I'm not very interested in that RSVP.

So, God offers me a special grace to get me back on track. It's my way home, back to my true self. It is the grace of contentment. He gives me the gift that my life is enough. That I don't have to fill every moment with some adrenaline rush, some energy charge from something new.

Last night the kids and I sat around and played a board game. Something that we've done a lot of over the past year. I've found that board games give me an opportunity to stare into the faces of my kids and see them for who they are- the gifts that they are to my life. In the pain that I try to avoid, they are reminders that God is close, that He is with us. Game night is the simplicity of life that I need to be reminded that there, between Park Place and Boardwalk, I can offer my family joy and that is enough. And they can give our family their gifts-goodness, love, creativity, wisdom, faithfulness, and peace. I once heard a preacher define joy as, "the feeling you have of being home." My gift of presence, my gift of stability that I am learning from my parents, my gift of appreciation and acknowledgment, my gift of a place of value and dignity in our home. My gift is joy. And that's enough.

MOVIE MAGIC

I am the biggest movie fan that I know. I have a couple of friends that I talk with about them a lot. It's not because we don't have anything better to talk about, I think it's just because we love movies so much. One of my friends and I have a standing agreement to talk to each other on road trips where we've made up movie trivia games. I always lose, but not because I've seen less movies, because I have a lousy memory. For some reason, I can usually remember the lead actors, the director, and a lot of the time the writer. So, I lose because my friend suckered me into games that feature his strengths.

I have seen all the Best Picture winners since the 80's and in 2003, I randomly decided to start watching all the Best Picture nominees to make my own pick. Last year I watched every picture from seven different categories and had my own award show in my head. Every picture that I wanted to win did at that show. And we didn't have any middle-of-the-speech-mishaps.

I'm afraid that I've turned into a little bit of a movie snob. I know a lot of people that feel bad to say, "That movie wasn't good." Like saying that will hurt its feelings. But some movies are just bad. I'm looking at you *Allied*. You can't build a plot around two people that are hopelessly in love and yet have no chemistry at all on the screen. I wanted to like you! You just didn't like yourself. Through the years bad movies have gotten worse and good movies have gotten deep. I honestly think that we are in the best place for storytelling on the big and small screen that we've ever been in my lifetime.

I'm not completely sure what it is about movies that I love, but I do know that it's an immersive experience. Which is easier at the theater. I forget about the day and submerge myself into a new world for a couple of hours. For an escapist, there probably isn't a healthier way.

Tiffanni and I spend every Friday at the movies. We've seen about 50 movies at the theater over the past year. And I have to admit, as expensive as it is, movies were made to be seen in the theater. Years ago, I didn't like going with her as much because there was so much pressure on me to get the movie right. We didn't go as often and for every movie that I picked, she got the next pick. If we sat through a lousy movie that I chose, that was inevitably two lousy movies in a row. Unless you like Nicholas Sparks.

Every week I get to pretend. My imagination is incited, my emotions charged and I lock fully into an experience. I travel to fantasy worlds built by comic book masters, relive historical events through the lives of yesterday's heroes, explore new planets, experiment with new technology, feel the tension of conflict at every level, cathartically delving into other people's emotions. And all the while, sitting beside me is the very thing, situation, person that I am trying to escape. It's a tough feeling to explain. Our life that we intended is the last thing that I want to leave, but this life that we ended up with is another thing. We stare at a giant screen filled with imaginary lives of adventure, while my reality sits in the peripheral just trying to stop shaking. The images bounce off her glazed over eyes as she sits emotionless, reflecting living lives.

"The biggest difference between real life and movies is that a movie script has to make sense, and life just doesn't." So, I reach for the tidy, avoiding the nonsensical, in order for life, if only for two hours a week, to feel ordinary. And the magic of movies offers the most appropriate way that I know to leave.

* * * * * * * * * * *

In case you care, here were my picks (apparently, I agree with the Academy a lot, mostly old white men...sigh):

Best Picture- *La La Land*
Best Actress- Emma Stone
Best Actor- Casey Affleck
Best Supporting Actress- Octavia Spencer
Best Supporting Actor- Mahershala Ali
Best Adapted Screenplay- *Arrival*
Best Original Screenplay- *La La Land*
Best Animated Film- *Zootopia*

THE FEET DOWN BELOW

In every nightmare that I remember as a kid, either I or someone that I loved died. It was either a car accident, or drowning, or burning in a house fire, or a plane crash. And each one felt so real. I would awaken shaking, heart pounding, sometimes in tears. I would tighten my eyelids over and over until they hurt as if they could wipe memory away. After the first nightmares, I climbed in the bed with my parents. Shortly after that, I would go get them and they would lay in my bed until I fell asleep. As I got a little older, after a nightmare I would climb in the bed with my younger brother. Eventually I dealt with it on my own, I think.

As I've gotten older the few nightmares that I have still feel as real, but I can reason with myself immediately after I wake up. "That was a dream. Everything is okay." I've heard that you can tell if something is a dream by looking down. If you can see your feet, it's not a dream. But I never think to look down until I die. And then I might not have feet anyway, so I basically died because I got sawed in half.

I remember Addyson's first nightmare. She was only two.

What is it about fear that it can invade the most innocent of us? Tiffanni and I weren't fearful people. We didn't speak about death or loss or abandonment. We didn't allow the kids to watch frightfest. One night, from her bedroom I heard a horrific scream. I bounced out of the bed to meet her halfway to my room. "What's wrong?" She just cried into my shoulder. How would a two-year-old know how to discern a dream anyway? Dave Pelzer said, "Childhood should be carefree, playing in the sun; not living a nightmare in the darkness of the soul." (From a book Addyson and Carsyn have read *A Child Called It*)

And that's what nightmares are: the darkness of the soul embodied. Those things that we most fear- whether we are conscious of those fears or not. They come from a place inside that humans were never intended to have. We aren't built for them. It's like trying to sail across the ocean on a unicycle- it wasn't built for that. Nightmares cause us to sink into the despair of that which misuses the imagination.

My family hasn't slept well in a few months. Huntington's has decided to invade the innocent. Sometime before Thanksgiving, Tiffanni woke up with a nightmare. "There is a swarm of bees in the corner of the bedroom. They're going to sting us." After an hour, I talked her down from her excitement and we went back to sleep. The next morning, I asked her if she remembered her dream. "That wasn't a dream. There were bees in the room. Still are." How could a child know how to discern a dream anyway?

Over the last several months I've stayed up through dozens of nights with Tiff trying to reason with her through all sorts of terrible scenarios. "There are ants in our bed." "Someone is in the room with a knife to kill me." "Your parents are singing

Happy Birthday to me and I need to go get my birthday present." "The kids are suffocating my grandmother." "Someone is trying to kidnap the kids." And dozens more. As if reality wasn't hard enough, now she must deal with torturous thoughts from her imagination. Hell knows no limits.

Huntington's is a trap. It tricks you in your body, manipulates your mind, deceives your emotions, and haunts your dreams. It raids every area of existence and then bombards those places outside of life. There is no sacred boundary. It answers to no one. It submits to nothing. Hell is its domain and it spreads its reach everywhere that it wants. Some days there are no bright spots, only spots. To pretend otherwise is to trivialize pain.

Nightmares exist. Especially when they leave the mish-mash of broken memories that encroach upon sleep and spring into life. I keep slowly blinking my eyelids and closing them as tightly as I can. Waiting for color to return. And to my horror, every time that I look down, I see my feet.

VOCAL CASSETTE RECORDERS

I loved the movie *Super 8* and the Netflix sensation *Stranger Things*. It wasn't even the stories- they were rehashed sci-fi go-to's with brilliant kid actors and a nostalgic setting. AMC has proven for years, get the characters right, have the best writers, and you can put a story in any setting. How about: teacher with cancer decides to make crystal meth to pay for his hospital bills? Or, an ad agency executive that gets paid to make everyone feel good about themselves, but never feels good about himself? Or, zombies take over the world? Get the story right, write well, and you can make anything work.

What I liked about *Super 8* and *Stranger Things* was the nostalgia trip. A bunch of kids running around in the 80's filming things. Now that brings back some memories. If I had to go back to the beginning of my life and pick an art that I would want to excel at, it would definitely be movie making. I get it, there's nothing like a good book, but there's nothing like a good movie either. I pick movies.

As a matter of fact, I had my stint. It was the 80's and I played with a neighbor's home video camcorder and wrote and directed a couple of short films myself. They were terrible. But they were so fun. The way that I remember it is that I spent an entire summer filming a Superman movie with my 8-year old brother as the lead. The special effects were nothing short of, well, turn the camera sideways and blow a fan in his face and he looks like he's flying. Editing consisted of, get the take that you like and stop for the next scene. If you didn't like that take, record over it. Who needs all of this newfangled equipment and CGI and green screens and stuff?

My generation was the first to have our entire lives recorded on video. I had a friend try to show me his birth when we were in elementary school. His mom said no. While all of the cool kids were walking around with giant cassette tape player boomboxes on their shoulders, just before a break dance battle in our parachute pants and jelly bracelets, our parents had a giant video recording suitcase on their shoulder asking us to, "Do that again. I didn't quite catch it." We were the first generation to have to reenact the monumental moments of our childhood. It wasn't long before television started offering a cash prize for our blundered moments caught on camera. More than once we tried to fake one.

These new kids are beyond spoiled. I get it, my grandparents thought we were spoiled because none of me or my friends died of polio or got trapped in a broken refrigerator before suffocating to death or got drafted. But these new kids think there's always been a time that we video chatted on Facetime and texted. We've gone from dufflebag sized camcorders to full 4k quality video recording on our phones that fit into our pockets.

Tiffanni used to say, "Can't you just pay attention and put that thing down." It was sporadic, but I was faithful to home movies.

"You'll thank me one day."

We filmed our wedding, our honeymoon (some of it)- we rented a moped in the Bahamas and I filmed us riding for about 15 uneventful minutes just before I propped it on the double seat, pressed record, and we reenacted a Baywatch slo-mo scene in the middle of January. We filmed the kids' births, birthday parties, Christmases, school musicals, baby dedications, water baptisms, college graduations, vacations- the memorable moments. And then I stopped filming.

It's obvious to me now why I stopped. I just didn't want to remember those moments anymore. While they were memorable, they weren't remarkable. Or maybe they were, just not the way that I wanted them to be. We always catch our greatest moments on camera, delete the rest, and file all of the memories away in a cabinet of perfect pasts. I guess I deleted a lot more over the past few years.

Not long ago, I asked a friend of mine to loan me his Hi-8 camcorder so that I could go through some old movies to show the kids. That was last year. For some reason, it felt like time a few days ago, so I called all of the kids into our bedroom. Tiffanni laid on her side, eyes rolling back, falling asleep. And the kids and I gathered at the edge of the bed for the fun. "What is it dad? What are we watching?"

"I want to show you some old movies of your mom." They froze their hyper, ADD, Red dye number 5 selves and stared motionless, eyes glued to the television. "This is Addyson's baby shower before she was born." Thirteen years ago. We were in the church foyer, filled with people that we loved. I kept making faces at the camera, Tiffanni chastising me in her

Southern accent. I had forgotten her voice. And it jarred me.

"Look, there's momma!"

"And there's Aunt Stacey, Aunt Katye, and Aunt Candy!"

"There's Grammy and Nana." (Yes, just me and the ladies. Not even my own flesh and blood brothers could suffer through with me. Neanderthal sexists.)

"Listen," I said. "What do you hear?"

"That's momma's voice." Carsyn stared intently at the screen. "I love her voice." It was lost on me until that moment, Carsyn was five years old when Tiff was diagnosed and she declined rapidly. The kids didn't remember her voice.

"Do you remember mom's voice?" I asked all three. They shook their heads.

We listened closely for over an hour. Laughing at and absorbed in dozens of scenes from our life. All of us captivated by the same thing. We didn't care about the setting. The other characters faded into the background. With bedtime long past, we wanted to hear one thing, one voice say as many things as it would.

While I believe in the power of words- the ability to give life and take life. The responsibility to nurture and discipline, to shape and to challenge. It wasn't the words that mattered this time. Say something, please say more things, just say anything. We each hung on every word and smiled each time that she spoke. I don't remember one thing that she said and I'd be surprised if the kids did either. But we got what we wanted.

Her voice. The kids love it. And I just miss it.

CINDERELLA

Every night that I can, the girls beg me to lie in bed with them and tell them stories. I'm retelling the same ones over and over and they won't let me leave. "Just one more Daddy, please." Who can resist "Daddy"? One of my go-to's is this monumental mistake of parenting that I like to think any of you could have made too.

Sunday afternoons are made for naps- especially Sunday afternoons in the middle of winter. Sunday clothes off, sliding into the cool sheets with a dozen blankets on top. Sleeping so hard and so long that the winter sun sets before you wake. But let's be honest, I can nap in any season, in any temperature.

We had just moved into our brand-new house that Tiffanni and I built in 2007. My girls were 3 and 2 and it was one of those wintery afternoons. We all laid down and I was asleep in minutes. I've always been a light sleeper and I was startled out of my sleep when I heard the front door slam shut. "Surely that was just a dream." I laid there debating, eyes refusing to open, "Could someone have just broken into my house?" And then it hit me, "The girls!"

I darted into their room and found empty beds. My heart pounding, I ran back to my room, threw on a pair of pants (why is it called a pair again?) and shot out the door. My guess is that every parent has felt that feeling. The one where you beg God to let everything be ok, "Just please let me find my girls." And at the same time think, "I'm going to kill them." I ran around the house, looked up and down the street, and heard a faint cackle. From my driveway, I saw them- playing on the next-door neighbors' swing set. Wearing Disney princess dresses, and plastic fake high-heels, they were sliding and swinging and didn't even realize that their hands and feet were numb from the cold. Their rosy cheeks would foreshadow the soon-to-be color of their behinds.

I'm a prisoner of the moment, my current mood affects my memory, but the way I remember it- I always wanted two girls first. Tiff and I only had girl names picked out those first two rounds. I never flinched at carrying pink dressed, pig-tailed, non-stop talkers in one arm and a blinged out Alicia Silverstone Clueless-themed diaper bag on the other. It was estrogen central there for a little while and I loved every minute of it.

Every night I go into the girls' rooms and talk and pray with them. My prayer is some slight variation of, "Jesus, thank you for my beautiful princesses, give them a good night sleep and sweet dreams." I want them to feel like a princess forever.

As a youth minister, a lot of event flyers and postcards come across my desk every week. A few weeks ago, I got a flyer for Winter Jam- a concert with 10 different artists at the BJCC for only $10. For the first time ever in life, and I've taken teens on hundreds of outings over the last twenty years, I thought, "This would be perfect for my girls. I think I'll plan a youth trip."

I never imagined planning an entire event with teenagers just to watch the faces of my daughters light up as they rocked out to bands that I've never heard of. I remember my Petra, Carmen, and DC Talk concerts vividly, dressing up to fit the part, to join the mood. I envisioned the girls in their light make-up, hairsprayed locks, and pre-teen interpreted rocker looks. But not my girls. There's no time for rock when there's a ball to attend.

As fate would have it, I didn't pay attention to the calendar and Winter Jam landed on the same night as their Spring Formal. They had to make a decision- rock out with dad or doll up with their friends.

So, off they went one way and I the other. Dressed to the nines, sequined ball gowns, carted in a Toyota pumpkin to forget the world for a night and pretend that dances and boys and music and make-up were how us adults would live our lives if we could do whatever we wanted. Growing up too fast for too many reasons that I can't control, it wasn't so much of a dad rejection as it was a childhood rejection which seems to be all too obvious lately. My baby girls aren't babies anymore and I hate it. Not completely hate it, but I would do the last 13 years all over again and again like Groundhog Day if it was an option.

Every dad needs a girl to keep him soft. To keep him from thinking manhood is about toughness and mettle, authority and machismo. But having little girls isn't about me at all, not about what it does or can do for me. It's all about the gift I have been given to deeply love, support, and assist in shaping the beautiful and tender, strong-willed and defiant, life-rich and creative princesses that God gave me- pink worlds and all. I'm very pleased with the young ladies that they are becoming, but today I'm most pleased that when the clock strikes midnight, the dresses transformed back to t-shirts and pajama bottoms, and all of the pomp and glitter is gone, they climb in the bed with daddy and beg me to tell them another story.

STICKING OUT LIKE A SORE THUMB

I just don't want to die a stupid death. "Did you hear about Jeremy?"

"No, what happened?"

"He was pumping gas and smoking a cigarette and accidentally mistook the car's gas tank for an ashtray. He blew up." Ouch.

Which is pretty unlikely since I've never smoked. But a stupid way to die nonetheless.

Or

"Did you hear about Jeremy? He was driving in the mountains and watching Netflix. He accidentally drove off the side of a cliff because he wasn't paying attention. He just so happened to be watching Thelma and Louise."

All of my life I've vied for attention in most settings. I can talk over people in school. Try to upstage anyone in a play. Compete at an obnoxious level. Preach. I like the center of attention when I want it. It just so happens that I usually want it too much. It's probably some need to be recognized and adored which I suppose many people want.

At the same time, I don't like to be centered out for bad attention. I was in science class in 8th grade at a new school in Florida trying to make friends with my irresistible charm when my teacher said, "I don't know how they act in Alabama, but we don't act like idiots down here." That's not really the attention that I was looking for- I never spoke again in that class.

Over the last several years, Tiffanni has been hyper-aware of the attention that she draws. She hates when a kid sits beside us at Dairy Queen because kids stare. Like, bore a hole into your soul. And they usually choreograph what they're thinking with their facial expressions. I've seen kids, eyes peeled back with raisin-furrowed foreheads, and I've seen kids with mouth snarls of disgust. I always try to distract Tiff. As clueless as she is sometimes, she catches all of the gawking glares.

I don't say anything to the kids. I don't even make faces back at them. I don't know what it is about being different, but it draws attention. That's why we all stare when we see someone handicapped, or a little person, someone with a deformity, a transvestite, even a couple with eight kids, or anything that is different. I saw Noah Galloway (the wounded veteran from *Dancing with the Stars*) at the movies yesterday and caught myself staring at his partially amputated arm. Dragging a stumbling, lumbering Tiffanni on my arm and staring at another "different" person- what an odd combo.

Two years ago I took Tiffanni and the girls to Melting Pot after our Christmas Village estrogen extravaganza. We had a great night with a lot of fun and talking, and on our way back to the car, I was escorting Tiffanni slowly, I heard Addyson scream, "Shut-up you stupid idiot!" as she raced by me and threw herself into the car. Just before I could fuss at her, "We don't talk like that young lady," I opened her door and said tenderly, "What's wrong, what happened?"

"Those boys were making fun of mom. They were laughing at her saying that she was drunk." I hate the wrong kind of attention for myself, but what I hate more than that is when my kids get the wrong kind of attention because of something they have no control over. Our world can be cruel and oblivious at the same time.

And that's just it, how can a person be so conspicuous, receive so much attention and yet rarely be noticed? Not noticed in the unseen sense, because they get plenty of that, but not noticed. Not recognized for their personhood, their humanity. I get it, she's different now, but fully alive, fully human. There's a reason that the nursing homes have empty hallways.

Someone asked me several years ago what my greatest need was, "How can I help?"

I told them, "Just notice Tiffanni, make her feel like although things have changed, she's seen." And my people have done very well with that. She still gets shower invitations, lunch invites, and phone calls.

Everyone wants to be noticed for their humanity, not for their uncontrollable differences. And Tiffanni is no different. Or maybe it's me. Maybe it's me that needs her to be noticed for her normalcy and overlooked despite her unique needs instead of the other way around. While I try to pretend like nothing has changed, it's the gawking that I catch in my peripheral that snaps me out of my unreality. There are a lot of stupid ways to die, but none worse than a death that no one realized ever happened.

* I know that many of you read this with a desire to be inspired and uplifted. Today just isn't one of those days. Thank you for loving us in the easy days and the days that aren't so much.

THE TRAIL LESS TRAVELED

I asked for my first backpack when I was in fifth grade. Equipment was pretty clunky in the 80's. The frame was made out of plastic and polyester and looked like it was built out of an erector set. It was a generation before main-stream freeze-dried meals so we carried the lightest food that we could find- basically anything that wasn't in a can. Except for sardines and vienna sausages- worthy of the can, not so much the stomach.

If I'm being honest, typically my goal, I hated backpacking. Not the friends, and camping, and sitting by the fire, and burly-man honesty- I hated the backpacking. Traversing mountains is hard enough on my own, but with a 30-pound pack strapped uncomfortably to my shoulders and waist it was miserable. Plastic frame imprinted into my flesh, a waist strap that dug into my hips, and boots that would have drowned me were I to swim in them made for a miserable hike. We never hiked at a comfortable pace, no, hiking is just like driving for men- there is only one lane.

But I kept going. There's a tradeoff that far outweighs the physical pain of trailblazing. It's what happens around a campfire. It's sleeping under the stars. It's unplugging from the deafening noise of the mundane. It's the conversation that can only happen between a man and a boy when the jetsetter group is far ahead and the slow group with the contraband canned good loaded packs are falling behind. Life conversations. The minimal words that happen between companioned miles. That life-giving interchange takes place as much, if not more, in Silence as it does in the verbal exchange. In a world that excesses in every communication medium, the trail requires the opposite. Listening.

After my freshman year of seminary, I stopped for two nights at a campground on the way home to listen again. I hadn't camped in years. With nothing but my Bible and a tent, I spent two days alone. There is nothing more arduous to a noise-satiated mind than Silence. Saturated in speed and busyness, tedium and distraction- Silence hurts. I think that's why many of us get so frustrated when we set aside time for devotional quiet and quit out of the difficulty. "I expected something to happen and all I got was nothing." It's why everyone in America has a guitar in the closet and only a fraction play. It actually takes work. Anyone can sit down, only a few can listen.

Ten years ago I took my first group of teenagers backpacking. Silence called. I knew that if I could just get them away from their noise-eroding real-life worlds, then they could hear. It had been years since the trail had spoken and I had my doubts. When you haven't sensed the beauty of Silence in a long time, it's easy to question if it ever spoke at all. The trail didn't disappoint. As we sat around the campfire that first night, sparks danced toward the sky, wood crackled, acorns fell and teenagers bore their souls. A symphony of soul-work orchestrated by Silence. God has written two sacred books- the Bible and Creation. They work in tandem to reveal His character and nature, His goodness and purposes and we work way too hard avoiding both.

Last weekend I took my kids backpacking. Silence called. They are convincing in their attempts to prove to me how much they love it, but I have my doubts. It might be the only space in their lives that they get my full attention. Silence does that. We only had 24 hours, but I am a veteran of the trail. "Don't rush, we're in no hurry today." We began our trek. I pointed out unique trees, solitary flowers, scurrying squirrels, chirping birds, the creek's splash, all a precursor to the song of Silence.

With Carsyn and Brayden pioneering the trail ahead, Addyson lagging behind with something on her mind, she asked between quarter-mile markers, "Dad, do you miss mom?" In that moment, it didn't occur to me that she could be asking several different things. "She's at home with a sitter, do you wish she was here?" "We've been away for a few hours, do you miss mom?" But the trail had already begun to speak and all I heard was, "I don't remember a time when mom was well. I know that you do- do you miss that time?"

"I do. I miss her a lot." And with that, the trail began. We make up games when we're hiking. They love lateral-thinking puzzles. The ones where I give a scenario and they can only ask questions in order to solve the riddle that requires a yes or no answer. "A man pushed his car. He stopped when he reached a hotel at which point he knew he was bankrupt. Why?" That's tricky for my kids because I've become a board game snob- they've never even played Monopoly. On this particular trail, there were markers every quarter-mile. Instead of them fighting over who would walk in front, I took the lead and let each one spend a quarter-mile with me. At each juncture, we would shift front to back, middle to front, and I would start or continue a conversation of either dialogue or Silence. Both beautiful, both purposeful.

After six miles that first day, we made camp beside a charming running creek, built a fire, and ate dinner. The kids pointed out the sounds to one another- rustling and crackling, fluttering and snaps. We watched the fire blaze and slowly die. Hot coals and moonlight piercing through the trees lit our chapel, revealing satisfied faces, contented souls- and I loved every minute of it.

There's something magical about the trail. It demands attention. On the second day, we passed a man by himself, talking on his cell phone. My kids gawked at him as if he was an alien while he passed. "Did you see that guy Dad? He was on his cellphone. Why even be out here?" They get it. There are sacred spaces that are easily desecrated by what we spend the majority of our lives doing. Spaces that live and breathe, speak and dance to the beauty of the Creator. Once connected, distractions dismissed, our souls are free to say what they need to say, hear what is hard to hear, and heal what is broken and overlooked. Through blistered feet, over-burdened shoulder straps, chafed hips, and sore calves, the trail is hard, Silence is hard, soul work is hard. But it's good.

43,815

I wrote my fifty-second post last week. One post for every week over the past year. More than once I woke up on Wednesday morning with very little sleep and no clue what to write about. Maybe it shows. But, I never skipped a week. I went through the chore, some days joy, of sitting at my desk and downloading my thoughts. And I did it for me.

About six years ago I wanted to start a blog. The problem was that I just didn't think that I had anything to say. I'm almost certain that I didn't. I kicked around several ideas before I realized that other people were already saying what I thought that I wanted to say much better. Then Tiffanni was diagnosed with Huntington's. And I didn't want to write anymore.

I really didn't want to do anything anymore. I didn't want to serve in ministry. I didn't want to talk to people about how I felt. I didn't want to sing, or preach, or write music, or exercise, or go to church, or eat, or laugh, or get out of bed. I did a lot of stuff, but I didn't want to do any of it. And I definitely didn't want to write.

And then just a little over a year ago, through some encouragement from my friends, I began to think that maybe I had something to say. And it was okay if I just needed to say it, no one had to read it, but I needed to go through the discipline of processing my thoughts. I needed to re-member- to take the fragments of scattered moments and connect them to some semblance of purpose, or hope, or sanity. Sometimes I needed to connect them to chaos, loneliness, and despair. But they had to be connected. I couldn't just let thoughts come and go without thinking about them.

I never told you about the Catholic monk from the 16th century that led me on my journey over the last year. Ignatius of Loyola. I discovered him back in 2008 and he and I have explored my inner life off and on for almost 10 years. He had this brilliant thought that God could be seen inside of our greatest moments and our darkest moments. Inside of the times that I felt far away from grace and the moments that I naturally danced to its rhythms. Through the Ignatian Examen, every week I worked through these basic thoughts: "Where do I see God?" "Where do I feel God is absent?" Every week, I've written from every angle that I can think of about our journey of life and death.

Today, I'd like to think through those questions over the course of a year. In fifty-two weeks, three hundred sixty-five days, twelve months- where is God, where is He not? Where does He feel close, where does He feel a million miles away?

A few nights ago, I sat at a long 9-year old boys' baseball game. For some illogical reason, this league has decided that it's time for kids at 9 years old to learn how to pitch. So, we watch 2 and 3 inning games, while kids learn how to take a walk. Over and over and over. During the Novocaine-less teeth pulling, I found myself sitting next to a black lady who teaches in one of the worst school systems in central Alabama. Testing is low, scores are low, parental involvement low, funding low, resources low, hope low. We began to talk about her job. Discouraged, she told me of her frustrations- a system that doesn't, hasn't worked for her kids. Her babies. I asked her leading questions. I wanted to hear her share her heart. Finally I asked her, "Do you ever feel guilty?" Tears welled up in her eyes as she uncorked her feelings. With a stranger. Anger, exasperation, hopelessness, failure. Unfortunately, I am going to make this story about me, but I don't naturally bring out depth and honesty, introspection and sincerity. I don't naturally exude empathy. It's not part of my personality, it's not my default setting. At least it wasn't. But over the last year, I've had dozens of these conversations. Dozens. She doesn't know my story. But she felt a kindred pain, someone who would be sad with her. I think. I've had so many people be sad with me this year, I think they rubbed off on me. Some days, people just need to be sad. Without sadness, no one receives a calling. No one fosters a child. No one marches for something important. No one feeds the hungry. No one visits the prison. No one gives to a single mom. No one changes. Sadness is good. Huntington's is sad. And maybe I could have learned that another way, but I've learned it now.

Yesterday, I took Tiffanni to her doctor's appointment. Back in January, we were asked if she would like to participate in a global study. She would be entered into a database that would be available to doctors and researchers all over the world. Assigned an anonymous number, doctors would track her progression in order to formulate hypotheses and then test those hypotheses against all of the people in the database. "Of course," I said. Anything to kill this disease. The problem was the evaluation. Each question made me more discouraged. I sat in the room, fighting tears at times, as Tiffanni tried her best to answer questions, mimic movements, and perform for the evaluation. It was miserable. It's easy to pretend like nothing is different, nothing has changed. In fact, my subconscious aids in that agenda. It has a strong aversion to pain and will lie to avoid it. But the evaluation was undeniable. She is worse. I should have been able to notice it on my own. I mean, I pushed her into the office in a wheelchair. That's the problem with reflection, you actually see what's in the mirror. A year went by while I was writing this blog, words on a page, comments and views and likes and shares and friend requests and private messages and little emoticons, and while all that was going on, she got worse. A year further from what we had and another year with what we have.

I laid in bed with each of my kids tonight. Brayden read to me. He and I sounded out new words (recapitulation-really? I'm supposed to explain that at bedtime? Thanks Geronimo Stilton you pretentious jerk). We giggled and I snuck in a few tickles between pages. He's a touchy, affectionate kid and kept throwing his leg over mine. Digging his head into my arm socket. I wish that I never made him stop. The girls tried to bribe me for more time by rubbing my feet and playing with my hair. I'm on to them. It worked anyway- I needed some pampering. Each one told me about her day- the good and the bad. I'm getting better at listening, at being fully present. And trust me, that's hard because they have never-ending stories, infinite drama. But we laugh and gasp, and I repeat back punchlines and consternations. "She said what?!" "No, he didn't." I've had to discover a balance between escaping and parenting. They are my sanity, and yet still need me as dad. In some ways this disease is forcing them into what should only be adult emotions, so I compensate by fighting hard to keep them young. They don't do cell phones (apparently every middle schooler in the world has one and "it's not fair"), social media, or boyfriends. Huntington's has stolen enough, it's not taking their entire childhood. So, we laid there and talked. I didn't have anywhere to be. I didn't have anything DVR'd to watch. No video game or Netflix binge to get to. I forgot that I had Facebook and Instagram. Besides, my friends only posts pictures of babies and food. Meh. I was enthralled by the allure of the most beautiful girls in the world. And I just don't know if I would have those moments in my other life- my ideal life. they might have evaded me for stuff. Less important stuff. But now they seem like serendipitous lottery tickets. The moments that might have gotten away, but now scream to be lived. To be experienced. So I do.

God has been close this year.

One of my favorite books of all time is *The Lion, The Witch, And The Wardrobe.* It's one of the most compelling, exciting stories that I have ever read. It has intrigue and adventure, good and evil, deception and humanity, magic and mystery- and animals that talk! A journey through excitement, and pain and loss, and excitement again. When the Pevensie kids arrive in Narnia, it's "always winter, but never Christmas." But Aslan is on the move. He is anticipated in that winter through every page, every conversation. The story doesn't go as expected, but ends with brilliance and hope. A year ago, I began to dream about writing a book. And for some reason I looked up the word count of *The Lion, The Witch, And The Wardrobe*. Over Thirty-six thousand words. It might as well have said a million. I laughed. And yet somehow, every week I came here and wrote. I wrote about excitement, pain and loss, and excitement again. And you journeyed through this adventure with me. You commented and shared and loved me with your own words. You encouraged me to keep writing, that it mattered, that you cared. And I believed you. Last week I finished my fifty-second post- a one-year journey shared with people I know and others that I don't. And I honestly think that I loved it. Thank you for reading my words and loving me with your time- Last year, in those fifty-two posts, I wrote 43,815 words for me- to reflect and remember, but I've loved sharing every single one of them with you.

CRUSH IT

I've never experienced writer's block. I have sat down to write and only lousy writing came out. I've sat down at a piano and tried to put two lines together that flowed and gave the feels only to leave frustrated and regretful that I ever read Dr. Seuss. But I've never really experienced that sensation of, *there's nothing there.*

I suppose that my real writer friends would laugh and think, "Oh grasshopper, just you wait." And my non-writer friends might think, "Well no, there's always something to say. Just talk about your week. Anybody can talk about their week. As a matter of fact, I've got a great book idea that I'm about to start writing."

I've had a handful of people over the last year tell me that they were going to write a book. Asked me for some tips. Apparently the expert bar has been set very low.

Several years ago I contacted a teacher at our local liberal arts university and asked for a meeting. "I'd like to write a book." She was so kind, gracious, and I'm sure had heard it a hundred times. Two years before that, I told a brand new friend of mine that I had just met in Canon Beach, OR the same thing. She was accomplished, published, and connected. "I'd like to write a book." Same look my college professor would mimic two years later. It's that look of grace and realism. I imagine that every once in awhile someone actually says that, writes a book, and it's good. So, there's this fraction of a percentage of a chance that real writers have to oblige because someone did it for them.

The other day I stumbled upon an article for accomplished people. Multitaskers, career go-getters, power-users, ladder-climbers. The article gave advice about how to fly at a high altitude in your career and life. "Set a five year goal and then crush it in 6-months." Crush it.

I really do want to write a book.

Like, really.

The first time that I seriously said it, thought it, meant it, was over five years ago. I began to call around to some of my old High School English teachers and ask if they knew anyone who could tutor me in creative writing. It was my subtle hint for that teacher to offer. None did, so I asked point blank, "Any chance that you would be interested in helping me?" I got all No's. Quick no's at that. Which some might think surprising because of my gift for persuasion. I've talked my brothers into dozens of things that were counter-intuitive to common sense. Nope, all no's.

Undiscouraged, I called the local university and begged into my first writing classes. Three in all. Three semesters of beginning a discipline from scratch. It was beyond beneficial for me. Maybe most importantly, I realized that I had a million miles to go to write well. That first assignment was terrifying. The second, not much easier. But I kept turning in assignments. I began to read "How to" books on writing and systematically apply what I was learning. And I started reading better books. Almost to the point of snobbery. Pulp Fiction wasn't good enough anymore. I had to read stories with depth, and arc, and characters- but not just one dimensional characters- I needed broken heroes and misunderstood villains. Genre didn't matter anymore- I wanted guts and brains and stories- masterful stories. The cheap sentimentality and lazy melodrama stuck out for the bad writing that it was. I wanted the feels and I wanted the author to earn every bit of it.

Writing became work. But not working for the man, punching the clock, everybody's working for the weekend, daily grind kind of work. It became pre-sin Adam and Eve work. Remember the curse was that what mankind would do for industry would be a struggle- laborious and toiling. Before all of the talking snake stuff, Adam and Eve worked and were fulfilled in their effort. They felt satisfied, content, accomplished. And writing is becoming that for me. I'm starting to discover my voice. Noticing areas of growth and challenge. And most importantly, enjoying the process.

Stephen King says that writing is less about creating anything and more about excavating. Writers, artists for that matter, aren't so much creators as they are archaeologists. That story, song, painting doesn't need to be invented, it needs to be discovered- hiding down in the depths of the soul. Longing to express. And it's that process that has been so satisfying to me. I sit down with little to no agenda and finish with a reflection that expresses a truth that I hold. Hard truths, easy truths, but all truths.

I really do want to write a book. And today I declare a five year goal. In all, that'll make ten. Ten years of purposed, intentional education and training. Ten years of discipline and pen to paper. But here's the thing. I have no need to crush it. There's nothing about finishing in six months that appeals to me. This process, this journey, has been too fun and challenging to rush. The writer I was five years ago is far less talented than the writer I am today. And I can only assume that the writer I am five years from now is more skilled as well. There are no shortcuts to growth, only short-circuits. If you'll stick with me here for awhile, we'll just grow together. Who knows, maybe five years from now I will have discovered that story that's down in there screaming to get out, dying to be read and heard and felt. And the last thing that I'd ever want to do to it, is crush it.

MOTHERHOOD

I walked in the door to tears. It's hard enough to understand anyone when they are crying, but Tiffanni is extra hard. She was inconsolable so I begged her to stop crying long enough to tell me what was wrong. "Stacey got a Mother's Day dress and I don't have a Mother's Day dress."

Tiffanni had just returned from going out with her parents. Their greatest gift to me might be taking her to the mall several times a month. I don't think that I've been inside a mall in three years. I can live the rest of my life outside of malls and never miss out on fun, contentedness, satisfaction, or sanity. In fact, I'll stockpile them.

There was a time that Tiffanni and I "discussed" what we would do on our off-day together. About every other one, Tiff had some house project, piece of furniture to buy, pair of shoes to scout, something that resided outside of the wheelhouse of what I would consider an off-day. Every other off-day was the exact opposite- a day of work and grief and pain and toil. My offers were walks in the state park, bowling, road trips, long dinners, and movies. Hers- torture.

Even her movie choices were painful. I dreaded the movies because every other trip was a ladies' choice and her pick epitomized the over-worked, baby-drained, mindless, popcornfest chick-flick. "I just don't wanna think today." So instead she cried. Not like eyes-welled-up cry, boo-hoo please stop people are staring waterworks mascara-stained somebody died cry. I'm not sure how she constantly wanted those kind of movies, I was always willing to give her the somebody died movies- just not from cancer- I offered war, sacrifice, and revenge. Nope, she wanted the rich guy that falls for the prostitute kind of persecution.

Avoiding the mall for the last several years has extended my life by years, but not that particular day. Tiffanni wanted a Mother's Day dress and didn't have one. I couldn't tell if she was mad or sad, "We'll get you a dress. You always have a Mother's Day dress and we've got a few weeks anyway."

Maybe I'm reading too far into it, but sometimes it seems that she is holding onto as much of what used to be as she can. There are ways that even in her diminished capacity, it's obvious that her motherhood-ness has lessened. The way that she would have mothered, she just isn't able to do now and maybe she holds on to any semblance of that.

So, she was inconsolable. For hours. This is a fairly new change for us. Once she begins to cry over something, that is usually irrational, she can't stop. I couldn't distract her, couldn't entertain her, couldn't get her to eat. Despair was all that she could feel. We both felt helpless.

Over the last six months, these irrational moments of despondency either happen during the day with a reprieve at bedtime, or they happen at night- lasting the entire night and breaking by the next morning. However, the last couple of instances haven't obeyed those borders. Encroaching on both halves of the day, they senselessly drain all lucidity from our lives. For hours.

When 9:30pm rolled around, seven hours later, and nothing had changed, I began to prepare myself for the long night ahead. Looking at the next morning's schedule, what would I have to cancel, what would I have to move around? What was mundane enough to function through on no sleep? In college, I remember powering through days and nights with very little sleep and loving every minute of it. But that was a tired caused by FOMO- fear of missing out. This is a tired caused by physical and mental exhaustion.

I won't pretend that I protect the kids from all of this. I try, my parents try, but it's impossible to hide. At 9:30pm the girls asked me, "Dad, are you coming to pray for us or what?!" Thirty minutes late, I lumbered into their rooms for the nightly routine. "What's wrong dad? Why is mom upset?"

"It's nothing, let's pray so that you two can get some sleep. You've got school in the morning and we're already 30 minutes late."

"What is it?" they insisted.

"It's nothing. Mom just wanted a Mother's Day dress and has been upset that she doesn't have one." And before I knew it, they were out of the bed and in my closet. With Tiffanni maintaining a low-wail, the girls were on a mission.

"Momma, you have a Mother's Day dress in the closet,"

Addyson exclaimed.

"I do?" she said.

"Yes, look right here. It's still got the tags on it. Oh, and it's so pretty."

Carsyn joined in as if they had rehearsed the one-act play, "Look at the pretty neckline. And the colors. This will look so good on you momma."

"And you can wear these ear rings," she pulled open Tiffanni's sparse jewelry drawer. "And this necklace."

"Do you want to wear these khaki pants or tights." It wasn't a question, just an onslaught of bait-and-switch, a barrage of sensory overload.

"Yeah momma, you'll look so pretty. Dad will get you flowers and we'll go to breakfast like we always do."

"You'll be the prettiest one in the whole building." Tiffanni's eyes widened, the corners of her mouth loosened. And I watched, dumbfounded, as my girls rescued my already-lost evening. Holding up a dress in one hand, earrings and a necklace in the other, they looked like a bridal team on wedding day as they surrounded their mom with love and excitement at 9:30pm. It took ten minutes. What I tried to do for seven hours, distract and refocus, they did intuitively. A choreographed dance, peddling anticipation and beauty with hand-me-down jewelry and closeted-fashion, "We've got you Dad," they said.

We got Tiff settled and I escorted the girls to their rooms. Back in the bed I couldn't stop my head from spinning, "Do you have any idea what you just did?" They smiled. Prayers and hugs and kisses, I returned to my room to see Tiffanni lying on her side, eyes closed, sound asleep, where we slept all night.

BURDEN BEARING

I hear pretty regularly, "I can't imagine what you're going through." And maybe that's true, but every one of us have challenges. I had a friend of mine who has battled cancer for years say that to me the other day. I had a single mom friend of mine say the same thing. Sure, this exact situation looks different for me than for them, but it is challenging nonetheless.

I rarely get preachy here, and this won't be, but there is this passage of scripture that the Apostle Paul directs the church to "bear one another's burdens." We are to carry the burdens of each other. This isn't a masochistic directive- that it's better for me or Tiffanni if everyone experiences Huntington's. In fact, that wouldn't be better- this disease is evil. He isn't telling us to divvy out diseases as much as he is saying, share the load. While there is no way to carry the disease, there are other loads that can be carried.

You see, if the disease was all that we had to deal with, then that would be manageable in a sense. All of our attention could go to support, focus, disease control- but there are a few other things that bring pressure. Life alone brings with itself pressure from relationships, job, raising children and all of their extracurricular needs, education, paying bills, car maintenance, lawncare, home upkeep, recreation, you know- life. And it's there that my life has been engulfed by burden bearers. People who lift, carry, and unload in a way that is incomprehensible. For so many of you that have lifted a load, you don't think it's much. In fact, you usually say, "I know this isn't much, but…" However, at some point, each load, each lift adds up.

For a couple of years, before my parents moved in, there was a lady who picked up our laundry on Tuesdays and brought it back on Wednesday. Every week. Folded, clean, and ready to be played in, grimed on again.

For years, people signed a list to bring us food several times a week. One of the best parts about that was we always got everyone's best meal! Southern chefs, cooking their best to feed my family. I didn't have to come home and open cabinets and cans, pots and pans- I didn't have to feed Tiff and the kids pizza and fast food. We ate like kings- redneck kings.

There is a lady that comes every month and deep cleans my house. Sweeps, mops, toilets, showers, vacuums, makes beds, hands and knees, sweat and toil- cleans. This last time she handed me money to go take Tiff to our weekly Dairy Queen date. Yeah, handed me money- to clean my house.

My kids go to the greatest school. The teachers are fully aware of our situation and realized on their own that my kids were going to get half-attention on my best day. From the principal to each teacher- they each get one-on-one, hands on attention (not the same kind I got when I was a kid). Private tutors. Private project helpers. Homework overseers. Test preparers. I'm not sure that the kids love it, but I'm knocked over.

Tiffanni makes an appointment to have her hair cut and colored every other month. It's not like it's easy to cut and color a head that can't stop moving, but her stylist treats her like she's a queen and she's pampered for half a day. The kids and I haven't paid for a haircut in years. We make an appointment, show up, get cut, give hugs and walk out the door.

Last night a friend of mine took me to a fancy restaurant. I was never one for fancy restaurants and one summer five years ago, Tiffanni and I went to NYC to visit our friends. We walked into a five-star, chef prepared place and ordered. For the next two hours, we ate the best food I had ever had in my life. It was like I had awakened to this new world that I never knew existed. A light went off and I said to myself, "Oh, so this is what this is all about." The food was amazing, the company even better. Relationships around the table are sacred. Who knew. So, last night we ate the best Italian food I've ever had where I relaxed and talked and enjoyed myself. An easy night with good food.

A friend of mine gave me an above ground pool the other day. You know, just a pool. Tiffanni does so good in pools. The water lightens her body and stills her movements. Another friend brought his bobcat and dump truck over, dug a hole, leveled the sand, and prepared the whole area. An easy summer.

A year and a half ago, my sister gave me a subscription to a massage place. I go every month, relax, and let all of the toxins out- at least that's what they tell me. All I know is that it feels amazing. I catch myself counting down the minutes until it's over because I'm so sad that it has to end.

Another friend of mine makes all of our Halloween and school/church play and production costumes. My kids have been flowers and animals, celebrities and cowboys, Daniel Boone and dancers. You name it- she's made it.

I have two young ladies that came through our youth ministry that come and sit with Tiff every week. They talk to her, do her nails, make her meals, help her do all of her daily we-take-it-for-granted stuff. They show up at kids ballgames, play board games, and cart kids around.

When Addyson turned 12 last year and was going into 7th grade, another friend of mine took her on a make-up spree. How to's and bags of make-up. Just another something that I would have never figured out how to do.

For years, every end of summer, my sister and her mate (get it), come take the kids school shoes shopping. "Get whatever you want." As if that's not painful enough, they take them all at once. I don't want to shop for my own shoes, much less someone else's.

I have a young lady in our lives that has committed to teach the kids art all summer. Their own summer school. Every week a project that builds on top of the other. And before you see this as just something else, art matters. In all of the ugly that is in the kids' lives, art reassures them that beauty exists. Sometimes it has to be noticed, sometimes it has to be created, but beauty is there.

And then of course, there's my parents. "Stability is important," my dad told me. "We'll be there as soon as we get everything settled here." And that was that. They left their jobs, their friends, their calling, and their empty-nest-we-finally-did-it-all-the-kids-are-grown-and-out-of-the-house-and-we-can-celebrate lives, moved down, and started over. With kids. We sit at my dinner table nearly every day and act like a normal family. And they've just about got me convinced that we are. The laundry is done, the dishes washed, the kids are at school, there's food on the table, the grass is mowed, the house is clean, my children are happy and vibrant and thriving, and the dog stays fed. And every bit of that matters when raising kids. The normal stuff gets taken care of so that the kids never feel abnormal. They have enough in their lives to feel different about.

So no, no one has lifted Huntington's off of our plate. It's still there, daunting and evil, over-bearing and encroaching. But when it's the only thing that I lift, and I obviously don't do it alone, it feels manageable. At least today. We'll make it today and I'm sure we'll get some more help tomorrow.

MAKING A LIST, CHECKING IT TWICE

I met Tiffanni in tenth grade, she was in ninth. She had just finished her first summer traveling with the Alabama All-State Youth Choir and I assumed that she sang like a songbird. But with words. When you're young, there are some things that seem more admirable than when you're older. Anyone that could sing captured my wonder and a pretty girl with a great voice was like a dream.

I hate to admit it, but I had a real list when I was a teenager. Not just in my head, because you can adjust those subconsciously to match changing values, but a real list on a real sheet of paper- loose leaf, college ruled. It was what I wanted in a mate. We lived in the South, so I assumed that I would be married within a few years, so it wasn't that big of a deal to think about marriage as a teenager. Maybe as a guy, but not as a teenager.

The list was pretty specific if I remember correctly. In fact, I broke things off with more than one girl because she didn't seem to match the list at the time. I made up terrible reasons that I'm embarrassed to admit now, "God told me to" kind of commandment breaking, using the Lord's name in vain stuff.

But when I saw Tiffanni for the first time, singing with a choir- because "can sing well" was on the list- my heart skipped a beat. I imagined marrying her from high school on. Which is an odd thing to say when you're 16, but I really did think I wanted someone like her. And the summer after my senior year of high school, I was certain.

I've mentioned this before, but when I accepted my first ministry position in 1998, we weren't married yet and the job was for a youth pastor and music minister dual role. I felt good about pastoring teenagers, I was unconvinced of my ability to sing, play the piano, and lead people in worship. "Are you kidding, you're amazing!" She told me. "If anyone can do this, you can. And I'll be with you the whole time." She was a brilliant liar, so good at it that she believed the lie herself. Which is the best way to encourage someone- you actually believe what you're saying.

So, we accepted the position and moved to Tennessee. I began leading hundreds of people in worship from day one. The first Sunday that I was there was the third time that I had ever led worship in my life.

Every Sunday that I led, I got a little better, a little more confident, and every week Tiffanni bragged about how amazing I was. Just so we're clear, I wasn't and I knew it, but I honestly believed that she thought I was everything that she said about me. Admiration from someone you love, someone that I had watched in awe sing for years, goes a long way. Every week, we led, side by side. She sang, I sang, and when she harmonized, I sounded ten times better than I really was. It was like going to the studio and adding auto-tune and reverb and studio magic and all that jazz. She brought the best out of me.

Last weekend my daughters participated in the Fine Arts Competition. Several hundred teens from all over the state enter a contest of arts- music, drama, writing, dance, design, photography. It really is a great opportunity to discover a talent sans Simon Cowell. Both of my girls entered two categories. Photography and Vocal Solo. They have a knack for both. An artist's eye and an angel's voice. And that's not just dad talking- they really are great. Their pictures were beautiful and their songs entrancing. All the feels, all the chillbumps just hearing them do something that they loved. Everyone should sing, but the best of us should sing in front of other people. I'm not sure that I ever had any business singing in front of people except for the fact of what it has afforded me for my girls. Singing gave me an appreciation of song and beauty, of lyric and rhyme. I've spent a lot of time with music only to end up average, however, I know what good is and I know what it takes to be good- drive, natural ability, and truth. I'm pretty good at two-thirds, but I see in my girls all three. You can't go through what they go through and not be able to tap into an area of feeling that can only come from deep wells. Trust me, there is little girl drama, but they are full of truth, deep human raw truth.

Every time that we get into the car they ask for me to play a song. They assign melody and harmony and sing a concert for dad. I sometimes play my music just to hear them sing my truth because it sounds better that way. It sounds real and lived and honest and true. True, not in the sense of facts, I stink at those, but true in the sense of what Dumbledore said, "It's a beautiful and a terrible thing, truth, and should be therefore treated with great caution."

My truth is that my kids now sing the song that my wife

can't. I can't remember a time that Tiffanni and I got into the car and didn't sing. I also can't remember when that singing stopped. It happened over the course of years and it happened all at once. Her voice slowly began to fade just as Addyson and Carsyn were discovering *Veggie Tales*. Singing and bouncing on the edge of the bed, every word, most of the notes, all of the fun. In some ways, lists are dumb. What I wound up with that didn't make that list was far beyond what I could have desired. But I'm so thankful that I stumbled upon singing, that I added it to a teenager's list of arbitrary preferences. Without a song that once was and is no more, I never would have recognized this new song and the beauty that it brings.

THE GIVER

There's a book that came out in the 90's called *The Five Love Languages*. The basic premise is that every one of us gives and receives love through one or two of these five ways- gifts, acts of service, physical touch, quality time, or words of affirmation. Each one of us has a relational love bank that can be overdrawn when love is not deposited, but only given out. The way to be our best is to give and receive love, however, sometimes the people that love us deeply are trying to show love yet we don't receive it. They are speaking one language and we speak another. It's as simple as trying to speak to someone in English that only speaks !Xóõ.

I've never been a gift giver. I don't care much for gifts, I don't want to spend money on gifts, I usually delay gift buying until I've "accidentally" forgotten that I was supposed to get one. Tiffanni on the other hand was a gift giving, gift receiving fiend. For years she would buy me a greeting card on special occasions after carefully selecting the perfect one. Apparently Hallmark had someone on staff from the NSA profiling me and writing limericks and haikus for Tiffanni to use regularly. She would hand the card to me and stare as I opened it. I've always liked opening presents and cards in private because there is so much pressure. As she waited, my mind churned with thoughts of how I could react the way that she expected. I felt like the groom at the altar when the doors burst open for the bride to walk down. Everyone turns to look at him to see his reaction to seeing his bride for the first time (except that they've known each other for years and just took family pictures a few minutes before). Cards and gifts take too much thought and work. I never reciprocate the emotion that was first invested in the choice.

Tiffanni would stare, I would pretend to read intently. She, content with her purchase, waiting on a simple confirming tear, would wait as I read. Except that I wasn't reading, I was more trying to figure out what reaction I needed to have. Was I to laugh, sigh, cry, grin, wink, who knows, I couldn't bother myself with reading when something so pressing that our marriage depended on it was hanging in the balance. Unfortunately, I've chosen wrongly as many times as I have chosen rightly.

I just wasn't a gift receiver or giver. Now, I am a black hole for words of affirmation, but gifts- no thanks. I'd rather someone give me money and I go out and buy myself something practical.

However, there are a select few moments of my life where the gift was more than an exchange of commodity. The gift embodied my person, my personality, my interests, my talents- the things that were deepest to me. I'm scared to list some of these for the sake of offending anyone who has ever bought me a gift, but there are a few that come to mind.

When I decided a few years ago that I wanted to write, my

dad spent days building me a writer's desk. He spent time selecting the right wood, the perfect design, the stain- it would provide the setting of motivation for most things that I write. It's sturdy, inspiring, and has an intrinsic magical component to it. Reflective words, sacred words, fun words flow from its hull.

I have a friend who has leather stitched and book bound me a journal every year on my birthday for years. I use these journals to write music, ideas, to capture thoughts, rough draft reflections, and to invoke magic. It might only be magic to me, but magic nonetheless. On every first page of every journal is the Joseph Campbell quote, "We're not on our journey to save the world but to save ourselves. But in doing that you save the world."

I have friends who have gifted me with a meal, a great restaurant with great companionship, great conversation, and a nice evening. That's someone who knows me. I don't want a gift, I want rapport. I don't want a knick knack, I desire meaningful kinship.

And that's the problem with Mother's Day. Not for me or my mom or even my mother-in-law. They're easy. I have three children that don't know their mom. Not their real mom. Not the mom they were born to, that first conceived them in her mind years before she ever conceived them in her body. She held them, fed them, played with them- nurtured every first-step, cackle, word, hug, song, craft. Every Mother's Day, and birthday and Christmas for that matter, they give Tiffanni a gift or a card. And it means the best that they can contrive. But it doesn't mean mom. Not their mom.

Gifts matter because the people that give them matter. And so there's a sense of intention behind anything that they give to their mother. They give "World's Best Mom" mugs and Happy Mother's Day cards, crafty trinkets and clever novelties, keychains and massage coupons and stickers and door hangers and refrigerator magnets. But nothing says Tiffanni. None of it reflects her now hidden personality, her disease masked soul. Nothing exemplifies who she was, the woman that I married partly because of how amazing a mom I could already tell that she would be.

I'm just not a gift-giver, but there are three gifts that are worth the world. Tiffanni gave them to me 12, 11, and 9 years ago. While they can't give gifts to her that reflect who she is, they do. They reflect who she is. Their laughs, humor, love, empathy, compassion, gifts, loves, looks, words, and lives remind me of their mom every day. They might not ever know their real mom, but because of them- my gifts, I'll never forget her.

WHERE THE WILD THINGS ARE

Reading and I have an interesting relationship. While I love to read, I am so easily distracted by life that reading doesn't get near as much of my time as I wish it did. I buy a book every week or two, but if I don't read it immediately, I forget that I bought it and move on to my next one. I tried the Kindle thing and have about 200 books in my collection, but I've recently gone back to the crisp, tangible feel and smell of paper. It's just better.

When I was a kid, I vividly remember a few books from the library like *Superfudge, Oh The Places You Will Go, and Where The Wild Things Are. Wild Things* was my favorite, probably because it's barely 300 words, but also because of the imagination of Max the main character. When they turned it into a movie in 2009, I was so excited to watch it with the girls. We read the book (because you're always supposed to read the book first) and then sat down to watch the movie one night. The girls were 4 and 5 and I found myself splitting my attention between the movie and their attention, laser focused on the screen, the images bouncing off of their eyes. The movie was darker than the book. Max retreated to the land of the Wild Things to eschew the brokenness of his life. I assumed the heavier elements went over the girls' heads, but when the movie ended they both immediately burst into tears. No warning, no obvious cause, "Why are you crying?" I asked, startled and confused.

"I don't know," they both replied.

"Is it because of Max or his mom or the Wild Things?"

"I don't know," they repeated. Somehow they had seen bigger-than-life puppets, explored Max's imagination, heard the voices of the Wild Things, but felt the heaviness of the movie and didn't even realize it. They were sad but didn't have the point of reference for brokenness from family dysfunction. Their insulated lives' first experience with grief. Like trying to describe the color blue to a blind person, they couldn't describe the new emotions that they felt. So, they cried.

Last week I went to a viewing for a close family friend's gone-too-soon brother. It was a long drive and Carsyn asked to ride with me. Her brother sick and her sister at cheer practice, the thought of piddling around the house in boredom was somehow ousted by the prospect of riding in a car with me for two hours, only to watch me visit with friends around a casket for another.

I took advantage of the impromptu date and Carsyn and I went to a nice dinner at a seafood restaurant on the way home. I could tell that she realized the significance as well because she didn't even look at the kids' menu. Just us, good food, and all the time we wanted. One area that Tiffanni and I, and now my parents and I place importance on is meals. Meals are sacred. There's something both mystical and practical about farming, preparing, and eating food together. It's that one place that my family can disconnect from everything, stare at each other and take enough time to just see what comes up. Unfortunately, when an entire culture fills every reflective space with technology and distraction, we actually lose the discipline of introspection and thought- both individually and familial. Mealtime is our attempt to re-connect, every day, to think, to converse, to celebrate, to laugh, and to love. And we're pretty good at it.

We stayed for nearly two hours and conversation filled every moment that it needed to. I couldn't tell you who we sat next to or what the decor of the restaurant was because Carsyn had all of my attention. And not because I forced myself to focus, because she hijacked my attention from the minute we sat down. She told me stories, asked questions, made me laugh, and exceeded her word quota for the week. Unforced, easy, natural conversation from my thoughtful baby girl- it was a beautiful evening.

On the way home she asked me why I never let her and her siblings read my blog. "Some of my friends and my teachers read it and talk to me about it." I didn't have an answer. I think it's less a conscious choice and more that they don't have access to the internet. "Can I read it?"

"Some of it is pretty heavy, but I'll let you read one with me right now." I handed her my phone and asked her to read aloud. She's a great reader and I smiled as she caught some of my nuance and tone, how she grinned at some of the subtle jokes. As she read through last week's "The Giver", the ending was heavy. I wrote about how the kids would never know their mom the way that I do, but that because of them I will never forget her. As she finished the last word, and before I could ask what she thought, she burst into tears. Like full on, wept. "What's wrong?" I asked.

"I don't know," she said. But I knew. I knew that I had held a mirror up to her own grief. Her own loss. The sense of growing up without a mom must be suffocating at times, and at others- numbing. Tears filled my eyes as I parked the car. Conversation was over, yet communication at its peak. And we cried together. Both for loss. She for the understanding that things are not as they should be and me for the realization that she understands that now. Now more than ever in her short life.

At one point in *Wild Things*, Max declares, "There should be a place where only the things you want to happen, happen!" When I'm at my best, I create those moments for myself and my kids. But more times than not, I am not at my best, so I can't create them- but I see them. I name them. I recognize them. I don't see them all, but I see just enough to capitalize on a once in a lifetime moment, a sacred meal with the most beautiful eleven year old in the world who just so happens to be wrestling her own *Wild Things*. And while we can't make them disappear, I can't insulate her from them, we can love each other through them. One conversation-filled sacred meal, one silent car ride at a time.

AN INDEPENDENCE IN STUMBLING

The kids and I stumbled across their baby books in the attic a short while ago. I forgot that Tiffanni recorded so many of the firsts in them. She catalogued each week for Addyson, and each month for Carsyn. Brayden got a few broad strokes, but he's there. I was always surprised to see how closely each child's development mimicked the developmental stages in the books *What To Expect When You're Expecting* and *What To Expect In The First Year*. My kids weren't as exceptional as I had anticipated.

Tiffanni and I weren't great about documenting every moment, but she got the big stuff. This generation has their entire lives on a phone screen- my kids have some pictures and a few videos. I might do better to somehow gather all of the video cameras and cell phones from strangers around the world that the kids ended up photo bombing. It would probably inventory their lives better than what we did.

I don't remember the details of each, but I remember the excitement of the first steps. One of the kids (the truth is that I think I've compressed each of their childhoods into one person. Three in one. My children, the trinity) went straight from lying, full body on the ground, and rolling everywhere to walking. Those first steps, for a year or more, were wobbly and uncoordinated. They spent so much time on the ground with plenty of scrapes and band-aids.

I know all of us have baffled at the idea of falling as much as a child, but getting up, dusting off, and continuing on undeterred. But walking means so much. It's not just duplicating an action of adults. It's the entryway to independence. The first action of autonomy. It changed everything when the kids starting walking. We had to "baby proof" the house. They touched and explored everything. We couldn't take our eyes off of them for a minute or they would paint the walls, pee in the kitchen pots, and toilet paper the house. Soon walking turned to running and skipping and jumping and climbing. Walking became dancing and jogging and running bases and riding bicycles and swimming and cartwheels and diving. And one day it will become driving and dating and graduating and walking the aisle and pushing a baby carriage. That first step opens nearly every door to the future.

I've fought for years to keep Tiff out of a wheelchair. It takes work. Lately, I practically carry her. The last two trips to the movies, we used a wheelchair. For some unfortunate reason, the movie that we want to see is always at the end of the long theater hall. It's easily 100 yards from the bathroom to the theater and that doesn't even count the walk from the car. I pulled it out the first time and she looked at me puzzled. "Let's just get you in and I'll help you to your seat."

"No. I don't want a wheelchair," she said to me. Talk about ripping your heart out.

"Me neither, but I can't carry you that far. My arms hurt from just walking into Dairy Queen." She acquiesced.

I wheeled her in, got her to the bottom of the theater seating and asked her to jump on for a piggy back ride. She laughed and I scooped her up and hauled her frail frame up the steps to our normal seats- top third, middle. There are rarely people behind us there that I have to worry about what they think about all of her moving and if we are too distracting.

I have slowly begun to use the wheelchair for long hauls. Like the ballpark or church. Those places that I just can't quite carry or it's too painful to watch her fall over and over, even if I do stop the impact. I've never needed or dreaded something more.

The significance of walking is more than just the use of her legs. Because when she can't walk anymore, she is fully dependent. Even in a wheelchair, she doesn't have the ability to push herself using her arms. Everything changes.

So she falls. Over and over again because it's the price of independence. There is always a price for independence, always a sacrifice. Hers are bruises and scrapes and cuts and headaches and body pangs and band-aids and soreness. Whether she knows it consciously or subconsciously, the next transition costs a lot. Every day she asks for Tylenol, every day she falls again. A vicious cycle just to walk- but not really walk, stumble. All of the possibility that the first step opened, the last step closes. It's a high price to pay to stumble. But at this point, stumbling is everything.

THE PRICE OF PRESENCE

I discovered food five years ago. Not good food, I grew up with a true Southern cuisine chef for a mom that shaped my palate. We sat down at the dinner table nearly every night of my childhood and ate good food. I discovered food that you go out and want to pay for. Up to that point, I thought that you just went out because you didn't want to cook and clean, or that you couldn't cook- I never had an issue with the latter. I don't remember ever going out and thinking the food that I was eating was any better than what we had at home.

Once, Tiff and I had only been married two years, a guy in the church showed up with a "hawg" already butchered and packaged. We stuffed our freezer and had to send some back home with him. He raised a pig just for us and we ate like kings for months. Ham, bacon, pork loins, ribs, chops, shoulder, butt- you name it, we ate it.

Tiffanni and I took our last trip to New York City five years ago. We were visiting great friends who invited us up for a getaway in the middle of our reeling. Tiff was diagnosed six months before and the denial had worn off for a number of reasons, not the least of which, Tiffanni couldn't stay still. As fortune would have it, our friends Matt and Nicole had made City friends that made the trip unforgettable. Nicole was friends with several actors in two different Broadway plays that afforded us great seats and backstage passes to the most magical performance art that I had ever witnessed. Also, they had made friends with a Food Network producer. I should say, they made friends with a fabulous lady that just happened to produce *Chopped*.

She invited us to eat at Scarpetta, a Scott Conant restaurant. The first course began with a wild mushroom polenta that is etched into my memory. It was then that my eyes opened and I thought, "Oh, so that's what the fuss is all about. This is what people pay for." All of my life, eating at restaurants was less about good food and more about avoiding dishes. This was different. Very different.

Last week my baby girl turned thirteen. Beautiful, spunky, creative, dramatic, artistic, talented, and full of life- she crossed the threshold of childhood into the land of insanity. The only good thing about the last several years passing by so quickly is that I know that her teenage, crazy years won't last forever.

The saddest part about discovering food five years ago is that I haven't gotten to take advantage of it very often. But this night, I decided to take Addyson to a fancy dinner with good food. She dressed up, make-up upped, and rode with me into downtown Birmingham for a fabulous evening.

I have worked on this evening for years.

By personality, I am distracted easily. I erratically move from one thought to the next, sometimes interrupting stories, situations, and discussions. If ADD was the thing that it is now when I was a kid, I would have mainlined ritalin or had an adderall IV. Luckily, I discovered it and have intentionally fought it. It's not an easy fight, but one I've purposed to win.

I decided four years ago when Tiffanni and I starting going to Dairy Queen, which would turn into a standing date, that I would sit, stare, and engage with her the whole time, no distractions. My phone never comes out, I sit with my back to televisions and people so that I am only facing Tiffanni and a wall, and I work at presence. Eugene Peterson says, "The men and women who are going to be most valuable to us in spiritual formation are most likely going to be people at the edge of respectability: the poor, minorities, the suffering, the rejected, the poets, and children." My objective was always just to give her the dignity that she deserved, even if she couldn't communicate well anymore. Some days we sit and stare, for an hour, and I make silly faces just to see if I can make the corners of her eyes shift. It usually feels like at least an hour, but I follow the self-imposed rules nonetheless. Dignity was my aim, but her response, her reciprocation was unexpected.

Addyson and I sat there, talking, eating, smiling, and enjoying each others' company. Two hours passed and not a second was lost. It was a tapas restaurant and we set a goal to order ten dishes to share. Each dish, cooked over an open wood fire, and I can name and describe all nine- barely missing our goal. I know what she wore, a dozen conversations that we had, every plate, but can't remember much about the restaurant. Toward the end of our meal, I told her, "I sure wish we could watch them cooking the food and see how they do it."

She laughed. "Dad, look right beside you." Ten feet away, we sat next to the wood flame grill. Like a massive pizza oven, the chefs placed dishes on large plates, inserted them into and then out of the oven. All beside us, the whole time.

But I missed it. And yet saw everything that mattered that night. Tiff, once again my tutor, I treated our daughter to a beautiful night that probably meant more to me than it did to her- maybe not. She had my full attention- I noticed details and nuances, outfits and dishes, conversations and laughs, even concerns and dilemmas- all because I was there. Not just physically, I was there.

My presence cost a lot.

I'll never believe that the outcome was worth the price, but I was there still. Completely there. I don't believe in an "everything happens for a reason" world. That's dangerous when we're talking about real people. But that night, after years of work, after thousands of French Fries, hundreds of blizzards, and endless hours of silence, I sat back and enjoyed every minute of my daughter's time. Her life, her laugh, her love, her momma's eyes, and I didn't miss much. That time cost a lot, but that night, for a moment, it was almost worth it.

THE BEST OF TIMES AND THE WORST OF TIMES

It has been a month since I've written here. Which felt odd because I wrote for 14 months consistently and never missed a week. I wouldn't call the last month a season of writer's block, but rather life block. The last month of my life, my family's life has been the most difficult that I can remember. And maybe I am a prisoner of the moment, always (see) using superlatives to describe the current season, which has its positives. Living in the moment matters. Except when that moment is difficult. Then perspective matters which eludes me of late.

Perspective is the ability to take a step back and reevaluate the current situation in light of the past or even in light of someone else's dire situation that eventually changed. Perspective introduced "This too shall pass" into our vernacular. She penned the silly, bathroom poem *Footprints in the Sand* and started the whole self-help movement. You're welcome Steven Covey and Tony Robbins. And while I understand the point of getting a fresh set of eyes, or backing up and getting a bird's eye view, or even the spiritual cast all my cares on Him, I just don't know how to today.

Yes, I've tried everything. I take care of myself with exercise and vitamins. My schedule is not too busy and I have others bearing some of the load. If prayer was going to work in this season, it would have. There's been plenty. And it's not like there's a magic amount anyway. If God was into formulas and equations to enact His desires based on our effort, then we would usurp His position at first chance. But that's not how the real world works, contrary to the television preachers. In fact, that's not what Psalms looks like at all. Thank God for them or I really would be completely lost.

So, I decided to sit down and write anyway. I connect with you here and have committed to not pretending. Also, when I am in a tough season, I notice that my memory wanes. But I can't forget these moments, as hard as they are, they matter too. This is me checking in. This is me remembering. This is me documenting all of the moments of my life- not just the Facebook and Instagram moments.

Don't get me wrong, happiness and joy and laughter and friendships are close. They aren't fake or forced, they might be more intentional (which could be a good thing), but I have plenty to be happy and laugh about. What's odd is that they spin simultaneously with my other emotions. Orbiting the paradox of my life that might not be a paradox at all, but maybe just life. I have found that there aren't really any moments of undiluted, singular emotion. It's a mixed bag of happy and sad, frustration and contentment. And that's what life is.

FIRE AND RAIN

I have a love/hate relationship with medicine. Tiffanni takes six different medications every day, four times per day. A different combination to balance her mood, movement, cognition, and motor skills. We know what each of the pills do individually, but what happens when you combine this particular concoction? The body is a brilliant machine and on its average to best days, has the ability to regulate itself. Tiffanni's body has a hard time doing just that, but it's not completely unable. So, we cram pills into her hoping to balance its inadequacies, and then manage the side effects of the first pills that she took.

A few months after her diagnosis, nearly six years ago, I went to see a therapist.

"I just don't have strong feelings anymore," I told her. "I used to get very excited about things, I would feel the giddiness of new exploits, excitement before a trip, I had more 'night before Christmas' moments. I suppose the good news is that I don't feel really low either. The pendulum of my emotions barely swings at all. Like sitting on a swingset and allowing the wind to give a push."

We talked once a month for several months when she told me that I was depressed. I managed my mood fairly well on my own, nevertheless, depressed. She asked me if I would like to see the "Doctor".

"It's probably time for you to sit with the psychiatrist if you're comfortable with that."

Pensive, I responded, "My understanding of depression and medicine is this: when we go through trauma or grief, our bodies respond for survival. My body believes that if I were to feel all of the feelings that come with what I'm going through, it would be overwhelming. So, it has shut itself down in order to survive and make it through each day. When it believes that I can handle the situation, it will correct itself."

She agreed so I told her that I wanted my body to do what it does, to which she gave a final warning. "I'm not a pill pusher and I only want you to do what you feel comfortable with. While the body is brilliant, it also forms patterns and habits. If you wait too long to correct it, it will have formed a new normal of not producing the hormones at the level it is supposed to. This is when you have to take corrective measures."

I left with a feeling of hope that my body was doing what it was supposed to do, but also a feeling of concern. I didn't know how long I was supposed to wait until I did something- there was this arbitrary date floating around that felt like a point of no return. I wanted to feel again, but I didn't want to feel everything. I wanted to be excited, and happy, and awe-inspired, and creative, and even sad- but I didn't just want to be very sad. For a couple of years, I carried this weight of a muted life, a life in black and white watching people live in technicolor. Lumbering through Pleasantville desperately longing to see red.

For four years Tiffanni's disease (have you ever noticed the word disease? Dis-ease. Something that destroys ease) was regulated by medicine. Her body never cooperated, but her mood and cognition saw little instability. She was bright, thoughtful, had a great memory, hopeful, and seemed to be optimistic. Outside of the challenges of her body, we lived a manageable life. But something happened last year. The medicine didn't change, but everything else did. Everything.

Tiffanni began to have delusions, hallucinations, and fixations. There were people in our house trying to kidnap our kids. Beehives in the corner of the bedroom. Bugs crawling all over her. People were trying to hurt her. Others, plotting against her. And the fixations were undeterred, sometimes hysterical. She needed her nails done, hair cut, a mammogram, to go to Olive Garden- you name it and it was unceasing.

With that we began a new search for management. The current medicine didn't match the symptoms anymore. And this wasn't an easy fix. She has had one to two medicine changes every month for nearly a year. Nothing worked, nothing penetrated those OCD like preoccupations.

Sometime last year, I decided that enough was enough. I needed to feel again. My body had protected me long enough and had probably formed some habits that were keeping my emotions from cooperating. I went to see a doctor. Just a Family Practitioner, not a psychiatrist. I thought that he would make conservative changes that would ease me into feeling again. He prescribed some anti-depressant that I can't remember. I used it consistently for two months when I determined that nothing changed. It wasn't working for me.

I went back to see the doctor and he told me, "In your case, there is only one other medicine that I would feel comfortable prescribing. Your particular circumstances necessitate a very specific drug, so we'll try this new one. If it doesn't work, then I just believe that God has determined that this burden is for you to carry."

Theology aside, that's a lot of pressure. "If this little pill doesn't work, you are doomed to haunt the doldrums forever." Theology not-aside, I just flat out disagree with that characterization of God. Which reminds me of how often we create God into an image that is manageable, understandable, and controllable. But that's another post.

I took the pill for several months. I never saw a change, a discernible difference in my energy, my mood, or my emotions. Either my body put up a stronger fight, the medicine didn't work, or this is my burden to carry- surely there are other options…

Tiffanni's body refused to respond to any of the medicine changes the doctor prescribed. I spoke with the nurse weekly, each time exasperated by the ineffectiveness of modern science. She would relay my descriptions back to the doctors who would readjust and tell me to check back in within 1-2 weeks. Every time, Tiffanni would have an initial good day, even two, and then back to chaos. We didn't sleep, barely functioning, slogging through each day just to start over again.

It's hard to describe the guilt of going to bed every night

feeling like my kids were parentless that day. The balance between caretaking, parenting, working, and personally staying healthy was impossible. It's like trying to keep four plates spinning that are in different counties- I couldn't get to them all.

I could tell that I was emotionally exhausted because I would catch myself having imaginary conversations in the shower, exploding into a heap of anger, berating someone or something with illogical indignation. That was a better alternative than actualizing those conversations. On my best days, I would levee the frustration long enough to complete my responsibilities only to hide the rest of the day. That is until the chaos began again.

Once a month I would say to the nurse, "Isn't there something that can just sedate her, make her sleep or tired, just to get through the most difficult moments?" The truth is that I wanted a tranquilizer. I wanted a break, needed a break. The whole family did. We all knew what was happening and tried to keep it together. The kids would fight and argue with each other without the self-awareness to understand that what they were at odds over had nothing to do with what they were fighting about. And of course it wasn't just the kids.

Finally, three weeks ago, the doctor obliged my request and prescribed more medicine than Tiffanni could handle. She was over-medicated. Nearly a year of lost memories. In an attempt to endure, my brain eschewed some basic functions and just survived. Sometimes survival is underrated.

For the last few weeks we have had no episodes of incoherence. Excitement is down, sleep is up. But Tiffanni is just there. A spot or two of life if you know what to look for and she squeezes out a smile with her eyes every once in awhile. She is permanently in a wheelchair and needs 24-hour care. But the kids are calm, fun, and acting like kids.

About a month ago I started feeling again. I think. Or maybe it was always there. A sense of time is a distant relative at this point. Tears and laughter came easy. It wasn't an onslaught of dammed up emotions bombarding my brain. It was more an awareness of subtle moments. Instead of this moment sad and this moment glad, there were some gradation in events. A change in hue. It wasn't just red, yellow, and blue- I felt green, purple, and orange. I might have even caught a periwinkle. I sensed more than the binary of happiness and sadness- but longing, surprise, interest, loneliness, anger, and awe.

The problem is that the renewal of my emotions have coincided with the most weak and incoherent moment of this disease. It's as if she has transferred her feelings to me. Loss and grief and pain and hopelessness and reality and lost time and loneliness and anger weigh a lot. I wake up some mornings before my consciousness awakens. Light and optimistic, only to be snatched back into reality. That's an emotional whiplash.

There were things that I was cognitively aware of before, but now I feel them too. I have felt a lot lately and I'm not so sure that I want to right now. I suppose my body has this under control. There are positives and negatives to feeling and un-feeling and I don't think there is a third way. You either feel or you don't. I've lived a long time un-feeling and gotten used to it. I think that I'm ready to explore more of these emotions, avoiding none. Because I'm not sure that I can heal without experiencing them all, feeling the feels, headlong into all of my humanity. Or at least as much as I'm ready for this season. Welcome back pleasure and longing and loneliness and focus and bliss and worry and misery and peace and empathy and hope- it's been awhile.

***

"I've seen fire and I've seen rain.
I've seen sunny days that I thought would never end.
I've seen lonely times when I could not find a friend,
But I always thought that I'd see you again." - JT

SUMMER'S END

The kids started back to school last week. We have an eighth, a seventh, and a fourth grader. That's recent enough that I remember vivid details about each of those grades for myself. About ten years ago, someone told me that my fourth grade teacher died. I was so sad. I assume that she was older, but I have her frozen in my memory as a great, young teacher. But then, three days ago, I found out that wasn't even true. She was fighting for her life. I don't even know how to respond to this because I already mourned her loss- how do you grieve something that you've already grieved?

I heard someone say recently, "The years are short and the days are long." Boy, is that the truth. The years of my kids being home are flying by. In theory, Addyson could leave home in less than five years, however, I've already concocted a plan for the kids to stay home awhile longer. Every passing year weighs on me. Did we take advantage of each moment? Did I make enough ballgames? Did I go to enough school things? Did I take advantage of every teaching moment? Should we have read more, applied ourselves more, vacationed more, laughed more, cried more? Did we eat together enough, play board games enough? Did we watch too much TV? Did I take too much time to myself?

For whatever reason, over the last several years, the end of the summer has marked a transition. It is where I reflect over the year, regret some things, celebrate some things, and evaluate Tiffanni's progression. This year was especially transitionary. It was an amazing year of trips and conversations, sports and retreats, school moments and relationships. It was also the most difficult year of the disease. Tiffanni was her worst and the kids were more aware than ever. I suppose that only continues. I sat with both girls more than once and cried about what they were missing because of her absence. Grieving a loss is hard. Grieving everyday, constantly reminded, newly noticed losses is brutal. And this summer was no different.

Out of all of the things that we did this summer, the one that sits with me, the one that I want to remember forever, the one that I have to write so that it's never lost is this:

Right after my sister had her baby, my parents were gone for a few weeks doing what good parents do. We were home feasting on what mom had pre-prepared in the refrigerator with some supplemental frozen gourmet. In a moment of creativity, I decided that I wanted the kids to each cook a meal. They could plan the whole thing and executive chef the evening. Appetizer, entrée, and dessert. Their siblings had to sous chef with no complaints or suggestions. Just cut the onion and be quiet.

Each of the kids was ecstatic. Cooking is in their blood. From my mom and grandparents, to Tiffanni and her mom, they get it honest. They went all out. Each trying to top the next, but not so much to outdo the other, just trying to be noticed. Food and meals are important here, so each wanted to offer their contribution to the value. We had so much fun in the kitchen, both creating the meal, which is easily as important as eating, and in celebrating it around the table.

I was so pleased with each of the evenings. Addyson and Brayden each cooked one of my mom's recipes. Carsyn found an old church cookbook and looked up my favorite meal that Tiffanni regularly made- Chicken Enchilada Casserole. A submission by Glenda Ann Cox. We shopped, prepared, ate, laughed, cleaned, and celebrated life. All while the ever-shrinking summer swirled by.

Here's to another over-too-quick summer. Another year of movement, growth, and progression- some good, some bad. Another year of laughter and crying, celebrating and grieving. Somehow grieving what we've already grieved. Another year of family. Another year of life. Another year of loss. Another year of love.

SACRED ROUTINES

I stopped using an alarm clock six months ago. After being sleep deprived for the first half of 2017, it was nice to start catching up. I have friends that can run on three and four hours of sleep, but I need a solid eight most nights of the week. Several months ago, there were days that I watched the sun set only to wrestle Tiffanni's demons all night and greet the sun rise the next day. Those days are behind me, but their memories haunt. Every once in awhile she will wake up in the middle of the night and wake me up to go to the bathroom and I'll be flooded with a thought, oh no, here we go again. But those moments never last. Terror false alarm.

When school started back in August, mom and I made a decision about how to do mornings. She would get the kids situated and off to school- lunches made, breakfast eaten, kids in dress code, Brayden somewhat coordinated, and out the door. I would go through Tiffanni's routine with her.

By personality, I'm not a routine lover. Spontaneity and adventure are synonymous. I like variety, choices, I hate to be hemmed into one option. It feels like prison. I imagine it's the way that my independence shows itself. On the other hand, Tiff needs routine. It makes the day go better. Her weeks are nearly identical day to day. What she wears, what time she eats, where she goes, her medicine regimen, rarely changes. So, we adopted a morning rhythm.

Most mornings, I wake up first. I look next to me and the only reminder of what once was lies next to me in that solitary moment- still. There are no hints of disease, no signs of change. We lie in the bed as the birds chirp and squirrels patter, just like we have for 19 years. She is sweet, and soft, and peaceful. I resist the urge to start the morning, and instead wait for a few moments to inhale this time. The time that once was.

We rarely started our mornings together for the first 13 years. She was a morning person, bright and jaunty, slamming cabinets, and coffeemakers, and makeup. It was as if she needed me to wake up, to join her, but was too coy to actually ask me to. I mumbled and shrugged into the day while she floated on top of it. Now I wait for her to awaken to begin. I have this fear that if I start waking her up every morning, that she will forget how to sleep. That the nightmares of last year will begin again. So I wait.

There is an urge to go ahead and get started, like I am lazy and the world is passing me by. And yet the calmness of those first few moments sets the tone for the day. Our lives are about patience now. All things take longer. Getting ready, eating, taking medicine, settling in, they all are exponentially more time involved. To wait for the day to begin is to posture myself toward a slower day. However, somehow I have grown to appreciate slower. Attentiveness thrives in slowness. I missed so much of my life when I was living it at top speed. I missed it on two levels- one, living a hurried life means that life hurries past. Second, living a hurried life without the ability to recognize the sacred, the important moments, made it go by even faster. A fast life of banality. Or at the very least, blind to many of the meaningful moments.

I stare for those first few minutes. The memories are real, the what if's even more.

She doesn't sleep long before her subconscious tells her that I'm staring at her. And her eyes begin to pry open. One at a time, escaping the night, her eyebrows go up and down acting as an alarm clock, long before her eyelids ever unfold. I greet her, "Good morning sunshine sleepy face." She slips a sleight grin. At this point, the rest of the morning will go smoother if I can get her talking and active. The next several phases of our day need her feeble body to be at its best for it to go well.

So, we play Faces. Faces is a game that I made up when communication got harder. Tiff and I used to talk about other couples when we would go to restaurants that simply sat across from each other and never said a word. And this was before cell phones handicapped our civility. Sitting at Dairy Queen every Friday for 90 minutes with nothing to say, or rather, nothing to hear was sad to me at first. So I created faces. When I felt that we needed to communicate some during our chicken finger and fries, followed by a salted caramel truffle blizzard meals, I would ask her to react for me. "Show me what you would look like if someone ran in here, masked, to rob the place." Shock appeared on her face. After multiple trips in silence, I laughed out loud and couldn't stop. She smiled and we had found a way to connect again. Sad, glad, embarrassed, something stinks, she gets me with that one every time.

If I can get her playing Faces in the morning, our day goes smoother. It's another way to warm up her body for the work it will face ahead. It also warms up her verbal. Most people don't understand her at all, but not even I can understand her words at first wake. Her mouth and tongue and vocal cords need a headstart before she tries to communicate. Faces gets us going. She doesn't play long before she says, "Bathroom."

Neither of us have ever had strong bladders. Years ago, I quit drinking anything an hour before a movie because I hate having to guess when the most mundane moment of the movie is to miss. I have to moonwalk backwards toward the door to catch the very last second of the movie screen before I sprint to the bathroom. But Tiffanni, she had three children sit on her bladder for nine months each. Those barbells did a number on her. So when she says, "Bathroom", that means we have seconds. Her eyes widen first and I know what's coming. No time for stretching, no time for cell phone checking- bathroom. Now.

One of the reasons that we built our new house is to give Tiff the best handicap amenities that we could afford. All of the doorways are three feet wide. The bathroom has plenty of room to turn a wheelchair. There's a walk-in tub with a long shower head hose. A handicap rail next to the toilet. And my favorite, a bidet. Which by the way, once you go bidet…nevermind. I have the movement from the bed to the bathroom down to a rhythm. How much effort I will need, how much effort she can use that early in the morning. It's interesting how something so everyday gets so much thought in my new world.

From there we make our way to the breakfast table. We've experimented with so much over the last several years and finally landed on smoothies. They go down easily and I can mix up almost all of her meds into the banana and peanut butter concoction since she has such difficulty swallowing them. Ten pills is a lot for the morning regimen. Before they got blended in, we would take 30 minutes just to do medicine. I've also learned that straws are nearly pointless. It's two swigs forward and one swig back- so I hold the tumbler and divvy the sips.

"Bible," she says. I honestly can't remember whose idea this was. One day early on we started listening to the Bible in the YouVersion app. Every morning we pick up where we left off. Sometimes two chapters, sometimes five. It just depends on how many begats were the day before. I don't know how many words that she understands. I doubt if she comprehends full swaths of Biblical history interspersed with sacred sayings, but there's a beauty in her request, "Bible." She reaches out her heart to a good Father that must meet her where she is. "Suffer the children to come unto me," He once said. And she does, all of those words.

A few months ago we were finishing Leviticus 18. I'm pretty sure that most Christians don't realize that chapter is in there. I sat there wondering if Tiff registered anything that the Heston-esque voice was quoting to us. The conspicuous mismatch between the voice and the words. Charlton went on and on with a litany of people, relationships, and animals that we aren't supposed to sleep with, to which Tiffanni looked over at me, turned her nose up and matter-of-factly said, "Gross".

That's one of the reasons that I love the Bible. It doesn't avoid the earthiness, humanness of where I live. It is not oblivious to the nature of my struggle, nor unaware of the brokenness of our breakfast. There are few put-together people within its pages. The sinners far outpage the saints. Those with doubts, crises of faith, inhibitions, dirty pasts, senseless sins, and prodigal failures line its checkered chapters. In all of its sordid candor in human repugnance, God weaves himself throughout. There are no pages that are too vile, too fractured, too crippled for him to not incarnate. He resides in every story and somehow, in spite of Tiffanni's diminishing understanding I know that she realizes that He sits at our table too. Intimately accustomed to sharing a meal with the outsider and undeterred by the lack of table manners, He eats and drinks, with us. A sacrament of blended peanut butter and banana.

Finally we round out our morning routine with a breathing treatment, lounging on the the couch in front of the Hallmark channel. Addyson was diagnosed with asthma when she was one. The first time that we hooked her up to the nebulizer and I saw her Darth Vadering the medicine, I panicked. Her heart raced so fast that I put her in the bed with us for the night. I kept my hand on her chest and never slept. The entire night. Now I hook Tiffanni up, tubes and mask and meds, and wait on her to finish.

It's usually during this time that she tries to tell me something. As if communicating isn't hard enough, now I'm trying to hear her soft-spoken, abbreviated words over a Peterbilt. It's hard to describe how endearing the vulnerability of needing someone is. When I would see Addy sitting in my lap, hooked up to science, she seemed so helpless and frail. Completely dependent upon me. And now Tiff, fragile, depleted, she lies there waiting for the fumes to do their work and I remove the mask. Not really waiting to do anything else, just waiting because it's the last part of the routine of the morning. She will spend the next few hours between cat naps, absently staring at Hallmark.

It's funny how doing the same thing over and over, day in and day out, hasn't made me want to escape. Instead I've discovered a grounding and certitude. I have so many questions about why and what for. Even some about when. But for this season, in all of its chaos and uncertainty, this morning routine anchors me to my vow. And the vow to love.

About the Author

Jeremy Sims is a husband, father, teacher, pastor, musician, San Francisco Giants nut, and Shrimp and Grits aficionado. He and Tiffanni have been married for almost 20 years and have three beautiful children named Addyson, Carsyn, and Brayden. They have a Golden Retriever named Fortinbras, named after a Golden Retriever from their favorite family book *A Wrinkle in Time* by Madeleine L'Engle. They currently reside in Alabaster, AL.

In 2011, Tiffanni was diagnosed with an ugly neurodegenerative disorder called Huntington's Disease. Over the last several years this disease has radically changed their lives as a family. This book is a collection of online posts from Jeremy's blog easyashardgets.com.

From Jeremy's author page on his blog: "It is my way of working through some of the challenges, as well as letting some of you into our lives. As an aspiring writer, for now, this is my outlet. I hope that you see the hope and beauty as well as the pain and loss and that it encourages you to love deeper and grieve better. From my family to yours- this is as easy as hard gets."

Made in the USA
San Bernardino,
CA